The Entrepreneurial Adventure

The Entrepreneurial Adventure

From Small Business to SME and Beyond

Oliver James

BUSINESS EXPERT PRESS

Leader in applied, concise business books

The Entrepreneurial Adventure: From Small Business to SME and Beyond

Copyright © Business Expert Press, LLC, 2023.

Cover design by Charlene Kronstedt

Interior design by Exeter Premedia Services Private Ltd., Chennai, India

First published in 2022 by
Business Expert Press, LLC
222 East 46th Street, New York, NY 10017
www.businessexpertpress.com

ISBN-13: 978-1-63742-279-3 (paperback)
ISBN-13: 978-1-63742-280-9 (e-book)

Business Expert Press Entrepreneurship and Small Business Management Collection

First edition: 2022

10 9 8 7 6 5 4 3 2 1

Description

This book will look at business and entrepreneurship. It outlines the process from understanding the opportunities and implications of having your own business and the opportunities and risks associated with scaling and growth.

Key aspects of the cycle that will be looked at are as follows:

- Understanding what is required to grow your business in terms of skills, funding, and some of legal implications
- Financial statements and sources of funds and how they will change with scale
- Day-to-day tasks needed to keep your business running and to give the optimal chance of success
- The importance of short-, medium-, and long-term planning
- Embracing the norms of risk, uncertainty, and change

The content will be brought to life using theories and supported by examples from a range of well-known businesses and business personalities. The purpose of this book is to make the readers think about their business and to consider areas that may not have been considered previously.

Keywords

entrepreneurship; business; start-ups; risk; reward; profitability; marketing; strategy; networking; managing change; decision making; uncertainty; stakeholder management; planning; resource and process management; consistency of good habits; research; market research

Contents

Preface

Entrepreneurs come from a variety of different backgrounds, and each has their own story to tell from how they started to how they became successful, with some inevitable and varying challenges along the way. Each entrepreneur and their journey are unique, some have started with literally nothing, some have previous business experience, and some are somewhere in between. So, it can be difficult to "Pigeonhole" an ideal entrepreneur—in many ways, it is down to the individual. This book looks at and explains the various areas that as entrepreneurs you need to be aware of at the very early stages of starting your business all the way through to looking at opportunities for growth and how you may look at approaching and managing expansion. This book outlines the opportunities, potential pitfalls, and key areas you need to consider at each stage of the exciting entrepreneurial adventure and growing a business.

CHAPTER 1

Introduction

A big business starts small.
—Richard Branson

Since the beginning of history, entrepreneurship and starting a business has been underpinned by the market forces of supply and demand. Across the world, all entrepreneurs look to address the demand for goods or services by providing supply.

A start-up business, which typically is started up by a founder or a group of cofounders, is a new business venture that looks to fill a gap in the market or address a particular need or shortage or a specific problem. While there are several avenues that can lead on from the initial start-up stage, it all starts from an initial idea and the courage to start and build on it and see the business develop into something to be proud of.

At the start of the process, starting and owning a small business can be as rewarding as it is challenging. Owners come from a variety of backgrounds and have many different reasons for becoming self-employed and starting their own business. In some cases, a small business starts as an idea that no one really knows about or believes in yet. However, it is important to note that some of the biggest and most well-known brands in the world would have all had to start somewhere. From Starbucks to Apple and Disney, all of these household names would have started from an initial thought that has developed into big business. So, each of these founders started with an idea and a vision that they believed in.

Over the years, becoming an entrepreneur has had an increased profile and has become a cool thing to do. It is no longer the case that we have two choices when we leave compulsory education—further education or entering the job market. It is also no longer the case that working for a big company is the only way to be recognized as successful. Starting your own business and making it a big business from an initial idea is, understandably, widely respected and admired. This can lead to success in itself and can also open the door to other exciting opportunities.

There is worldwide attention on high-profile entrepreneurs, for example, Elon Musk, Bill Gates, Sara Blakely, Mark Zuckerberg, Arianna Huffington, Hilary Devey, Mark Cuban, Kevin O'Leary, Deborah Meaden, and Sir Richard Branson. Each has their own individual story, motivation, and subsequent success story and that in turn will have inspired others to take this path.

There are also a number of mainstream television shows that have hugely increased the profile of entrepreneurship and encourage the idea of individuals starting their own enterprise, for example, Dragon's Den, the Apprentice, Shark Tank, and Undercover boss. With the huge viewing figures across the world and the emergence and the fundamental and critical importance of social media, both the judges and contestants can "self-market" and massively increase their individual profiles and their business interests. Furthermore, taking part in these shows in turn can lead to life-changing opportunities for new entrepreneurs, not just in terms of a cash injection, but gaining an increased personal profile and the benefit of working with a successful and experienced entrepreneur.

These factors have all contributed to a shift in profile about starting your own business and entrepreneurship, making it a positive and viable choice for individuals who may not have considered this path previously.

Individuals from many different backgrounds have become entrepreneurs, and each has a fascinating story to tell about the why and the how they decided to take the first step into entrepreneurship and what they subsequently chose to do. There are many skills and competencies that an entrepreneur will possess. However, it is important to remember that the definition of an entrepreneur is very broad. Some people would say that entrepreneurs are people that take risks, others may say that entrepreneurs start and build businesses, whereas others will say it's a mixture of different factors. There is also a school of thought that says people can in some ways be recognized as entrepreneurs while working for a company as an employee, an example being someone who runs their own large area of a big company. While it is fair and reasonable to say that each person who has become a successful entrepreneur will have their individual traits and skillset, there are some core skills that you would expect to see in an entrepreneur:

- *Knowledge:* This encompasses business and entrepreneurial knowledge as well as opportunity and venture-specific knowledge. Specifically, this will include knowledge of how business works, the day-to-day running of a business, and knowledge about the type of business you are involved with and the type of marketplace you will be operating in. These skills will serve you well whether you are doing your research in the early stages or are doing your research when considering expansion. Doing thorough research and understanding these key concepts is vital and supports and underpins sensible, balanced, and well-informed decisions.
- *Personality traits:* Examples of classic entrepreneurial personality traits are optimism, vision, initiative, persistence, and drive; recognizing potential, emotional intelligence; and taking risks. The last skill, taking risks, can be tricky to define and a misconception can be that you must enjoy taking risks to be an entrepreneur. That is debatable, a more accurate way of describing it may be, having an understanding that there is an element risk in various parts of the entrepreneurial journey.
- *Interpersonal skills:* Examples include communication, listening skills, being ethical, motivation, being a role model, and having a positive personal brand and building a positive employer brand. It is skills like these that underpin important business talents such as networking and negotiating.
- *Creative and critical thinking:* Examples include problem solving, creative thinking, and recognizing opportunity. These skills underpin some of the aspects of the start-up stage and day-to-day operations.
- *Practical skills:* Examples include planning and organizing, understanding metrics, decision making, and setting goals. Skills like these underpin some of the important aspects involved in the day-to-day operations and running of a business as well as short- and long-term planning.

Some of the aforementioned skills can be skills that you have learned through life experience, and they do not necessarily have to come from a business context (or in some cases not even a work context). These are also known as transferrable skills and you may have them without realizing. A bit of research on different high-profile entrepreneurs show that there is not a stringent path as such; many different people from different backgrounds have successfully built successful businesses. It is worth noting that it is probably rare that any entrepreneur has knowledge or expertise in all of these areas, particularly to begin with or in the early stages. We all have to start somewhere, and as in all walks of life, skills can be learned on the job and through life or work experience. And as in many parts of life, starting and running your own business is a learning experience and no matter what your competency/knowledge level is at the various stages of the journey; there will always be skills and lessons to be learnt as you go along. It is likely that an entrepreneur is always learning and is always seeking new knowledge as different challenges appear.

Nonetheless, having some of these skills and competencies could make starting and running your own business a good choice.

In addition to skills and competencies and the potential increased profile and opportunities for entrepreneurs, there are many other factors that make starting your own business and becoming an entrepreneur an attractive option:

- *Deciding to look for a new challenge:* At times in life, you may wish to seek a new challenge or to become a better version of yourself. This could be due to a number of factors, for example, you may feel underutilized, undervalued, unhappy, or that you are not fulfilling your potential in some way. Whether you choose to do so, or it is forced to make the decision due to factors outside of your control, having something new to focus on can be invigorating and provide the opportunity for a new challenge and a fresh start. While any decision you make and the consequences of that decision have to be carefully weighed up, starting your own business can be the very opportunity and new challenge you are looking for. As this book will cover, becoming an entrepreneur will have its challenges and embracing and facing them will be one of the key factors in making your own business a success.

- *Pursuing a passion:* Whether you run your own business and it is an area that you are passionate about or by definition you are passionate about your business because it's yours and you want it to succeed, the hard work needed will be that much easier as you are pursuing a passion. With hard work and a bit of luck, there is a huge variety of concepts that can be made into a viable business that can be expanded. As is sometimes said, "if you love what you do, you will never work a day in your life again."

- *Being inspired by other entrepreneurs:* Successful people inspire other people to become successful. Entrepreneurs can learn from the stories of other successful entrepreneurs, and if they choose to start the journey, meet and network with people who have made their entrepreneurial journey a success. Learning from the experience and expertise of others who have "been there and done that" is an important part of the process. Seeing someone who has made millions after starting with nothing is inspiring for many new entrepreneurs who aspire to achieve the same.

- *Not being afraid of risk:* Entrepreneurs tend to like risk, and ultimately, whatever type of business you have, there will be different elements and various levels of potential risk to that venture. However, the level of risk is something that has to be fully researched, measured, and understood, to make sure an informed choice can be made. Ultimately, it makes sense to have a balance of risk, pragmatism, and realism. Aspiring entrepreneurs have ideas, put them in to action and watch them develop into something.

- *Controlling your own destiny:* As an entrepreneur, you are your own boss in a lot of ways. This is a mixture of liberating, empowering, and challenging. That means in terms of running the business, you answer to yourself, set your own hours, and manage your own workload. When you work for yourself and you achieve something, you are likely to be more fulfilled as you have achieved it for and by yourself. So you ultimately take charge and do it your own way, rather than being an employee and feeling like a cog in a large business. That said, while you answer to yourself in terms of running the business, you also answer to clients and customers, who ultimately will be paying you for what you offer. They will expect a high-quality good or service at a reasonable price. So, you are accountable, and you have to deliver.

- *Making a valuable contribution to the economy:* The role small business plays in an economy and the value they add can sometimes be underestimated. In some ways because they start small, they can be overshadowed by the news coverage that their larger counterparts get and don't take the revenues of larger firms. That said, while they may not make the same big revenues, that is not to say that they don't add value. If they are set up in business-friendly countries, with sensible tax structures and regulations, small business and start-ups can make a big contribution to a country's economy as well as their local area. Small business can give people the opportunity to have fulfilling employment, achieve financial independence, encourage innovation, and also boost employment, by employing local people, who may be not be working for larger businesses. A thriving small business will also generate more revenue and therefore pay more taxes to boost government resources. And ultimately, if a number of factors fall into place, what starts as a small business over time can expand and become a big business.

- *It can open doors to other opportunities:* As your business goes from start-up to becoming established and potentially expanding, there is likely to be external opportunities that arise. This could be in areas such as keynote speaking, judging on business award panels, nonexecutive director or advisory roles, or taking part in business TV shows. However, these sorts of things give an entrepreneur a platform for increased profile and in some cases another source of income. There are also things that can be done to give back. For example, this could be volunteering and mentoring for a charity or giving careers talks or mock job interviews at local schools or youth clubs.

- *Lack of any other viable alternatives:* In certain cases, due to a variety of reasons, some people are left with starting their own business as their only realistic choice. It may be the case that working for someone else is not available, not suitable, or undesirable. Other factors could be due to unforeseen or uncontrollable circumstances, such as economic and job market conditions, previous work experience, unexpected sudden job loss, and education.

This book looks to outline the many aspects of running your own business and opportunities and options for expansion. The good practice and consistency of good habits you need to have to maximize your chances of succeeding will also be covered. This book also looks at the various opportunities that entrepreneurship can lead to, the types of challenges you may come across, the pitfalls you could face, and the reality, practicality, and potential rewards of the entrepreneurial adventure.

I never dreamed about success, I worked for it.
—Estee Lauder

CHAPTER 2

Is This Option Right for You?

Every success story is a tale of constant adaption, revision and change.
—Richard Branson

While being an entrepreneur is in the mainstream, it is not always straightforward. Being your own boss is very empowering and can be very rewarding, but having your own business comes with a great deal of responsibility. Throughout the entrepreneurial journey, there are many lessons to be learned, decisions to be made, and factors to be understood and considered. In almost all cases, this will be reoccurring. So, it is vital to do your research and make an informed decision before going for it and taking the plunge.

There are potentially massive rewards and opportunities that come from starting and running your own business. However, there are a lot of practicalities and realities to it as well. In all honesty, it is a matter of continually weighing up the benefits and risks and making a clear and informed decision on how to continually progress, improve, and move forward.

Having a business plan is important at the early stage. There are many areas to consider and covering the bases at the first instance will mean that you have done some research and have an informed idea of how to start, build, and make a success of starting your own business.

In a nutshell, a business plan gives an outline of what your business will do, the market it will operate in, and how it aims to make money. This will ultimately outline and illustrate why your business will be a success.

Your business plan is a template, a foundation to build on, and offers a structure to work to. This can be referred back to at any time, and this could be useful at certain times in the entrepreneurial journey.

Broadly speaking, a sound business plan will:

- *Clearly and succinctly clarify your business idea:* It is important to keep things simple. (Or certainly not to make things sound needlessly complicated!) Your business idea should be easy to explain, so that anyone can understand what you are planning to achieve.
- *Show an awareness of potential problems and how they can be mitigated or addressed:* Be honest and open about issues that may arise, all businesses will encounter issues, and showing an awareness and appreciation of this is a good thing.
- *Set clear, sensible, and measurable goals:* Using SMART (Specific, Measurable, Achievable, Relevant, Timely) objectives is useful here.
- *Show how and when progress will be measured:* Set milestones for what you want to achieve and be clear about how you will measure success. Examples of how you could measure success could be by net profit, turnover, or number of customers.

The types of areas to consider and include will be discussed in this chapter.

What Is Your Business?

A new business can range from an idea to introduce something completely new or something that is already out there that the new business can deliver more effectively. Both are valid ways to start, and both come with different benefits and risks. Ultimately, at some time in the entrepreneurial journey, you are going to have to be prepared to take a risk but understanding the level of risk associated with your particular idea is a key starting point. This also informs any future decisions about expanding. While all businesses can be expanded, some models could be considered more "expansion friendly" than others.

Different Types of Business

Once you have decided on what product or service you offer, another important consideration is the type of business model you wish to use. In essence, how your business will run. This is important to consider not only in the start-up stage but also in terms of if and how you will wish to expand in future.

There are a number of different business models to consider, as shown in the following.

Sole proprietor: This type of business is owned and operated by one person and can be named after the owner or be given a fictitious name. Generally, this is recognized as the simplest and most common business type out there, as it is relatively easy to set up and taxation is also quite simple as it is calculated using income earned from the owner. However, a disadvantage of this model is the sole proprietor is responsible for everything the business does and there is no separation of assets and liabilities and is not a legal entity. Meaning the sole proprietor is responsible for any debts incurred by the business.

Examples of a sole proprietor could be a small home-based web business or a trade business such as a handyman, electrician, or plumber.

Partnership: This is a business where two or more people join forces and work together to start a business or a trade. Each person contributes resources, skills, or labor as well as potentially money and property and would therefore expect a share in business profits or losses. This business model is similar to a sole proprietorship as the business is not a separate entity from the owners, who have the responsibility for any business debts.

Some partnerships include individuals who all work for the business, whereas some partnerships include individuals with a more limited input into the business.

Examples of partnerships could be lawyers, accountants, or dentists.

Company: A company is a legal entity that is set up to sell goods and services to make money. A company is made up of an association of persons carrying out a commercial or industrial enterprise, but in this case, the company is a separate entity from its owners. Companies are owned by shareholders who each put an amount of money into a central pool. The pool of capital could then be added to by other forms of finance such as external investment or borrowing.

A company can be organized in a number of different ways for financial and tax liabilities depending on the relevant laws in the country it operates. It is that and the type of business that will determine the best structure to use.

SME: This acronym stands for small- or medium-sized enterprise with fewer than 250 employees. With this umbrella, there are three categories: medium-sized, small, and micro businesses. These categories are defined by number of employees and turnover. In the United Kingdom, SMEs make up around 99.9 percent of all businesses, as a result making a massive contribution to the economy.

Cooperative: These are businesses that are owned and controlled by its members. This, for example, can be staff, customers, suppliers, or any combination of these stakeholders. In this model, stakeholders have an equal say in how the business is run and members chose what to do with company profits, be it reinvesting into the business, giving to the community, or sharing among members.

Limited liability companies (LLCs): This is a corporate structure in the United States and a private company and business structure that combines the traits of a sole proprietorship and a company. In this business structure, owners are not personally liable for the company debts or liabilities. Most entities can form this business structure including individuals and corporations. LLCs do not pay taxes; their profits and losses are passed through to members who declare this via their personal tax returns.

Franchise: This is where an agreement or license agreement is entered into by two parties: the franchisor and franchisee. Franchises are where licensing arrangements are made where an individual can produce and trade under a well-known brand in a particular industry or certain area. This entails using another company's business model and name to establish your own business. The advantage of this model is working for yourself alongside the reputation and established business of a larger organization.

Some of the most well-known brands in shopping centers are franchises. These cover a number of different industries, for example, Starbucks,

Action Coach, McDonalds, Papa John's, Subway, and, Europcar. All are well-known brands in their own right, and while there are several criteria to meet to become a franchisee, which will differ per opportunity, this is an attractive option to some entrepreneurs. This is due to the support the franchisor can provide and working with an already established brand. In these cases, you are not going to have to convince customers of the brand as it already has a reputation.

Criteria can include previous experience requirements and capital. For example, according to the Starbucks website, franchise requirements include £500k of demonstrated liquid assets and evidence of previous food and beverage experience. In return, Starbucks has a comprehensive franchise support program, including training, consultation, and new products. That is in addition to the advantage of having one of the best-known brand names to trade under.

Why Have You Decided to Start Your Own Business?

As we covered in Chapter 1, there are many reasons that an individual may decide to start their own business.

This can be a mixture of either you wanting to undertake the challenge of starting your own business, for example, wanting a new challenge or pursuing a passion. In some cases, the situation may have been forced on you, for example, being made redundant.

You may also decide to start your own business because your current or previous job is in an industry where the hours are particularly antisocial, and you want to have a more positive work–life balance. (As we will cover later, though, having your own business is by no means a guarantee of this.)

You may also be motivated by seeing others succeed and having your own business can be a platform for this to happen, either creating job opportunities and employment as you grow your business or by giving back—perhaps through mentoring, giving career talks at schools, or supporting a charity.

When making decisions about what to do next, it is worth revisiting your reasons and motivations for starting in the first place.

What Do You Need to Start and Expand a Business?

At the beginning of the entrepreneurial journey, there are a number of things that you will need to do.

One of the first things to do is decide what to name your business. A clear and powerful name can be an enormous help when it comes to branding and marketing. In the same way, a poor choice of name, which does not connect with customers or is open to legal challenge, can cause unwanted and avoidable difficulties.

When considering what to name your business, there are a number of key areas to consider:

- *Brainstorm:* Thinking about what your business stands for, your product, or service and how you want to deliver it is a good starting point to pinpointing what you want to call your business.
- *Don't pick a name that limits what your business does:* Ideally, you would avoid having a name that limits your business to a specific product or city. (This is particularly important when thinking about future expansion.)
- *Avoid names that are difficult to spell:* This will lead to customers potentially finding it difficult to find your business online.
- *Do thorough Internet research:* This is to avoid choosing a name that someone else may be using. Having the same or a similar name to someone else's business will only lead to potential unwanted complications in the future.
- *Check if the domain name is available:* One you are getting close to picking a name, it's worth checking if the .com domain is available. It is important to check that you can use that business name on the social media sites you may be planning to use. This is a key consideration as you don't want to go through the process of picking a name and subsequently discovering that you can't use it as your domain name. (Setting up a website and social media is covered in more detail in Chapter 7.)

- *Do a trademark search:* To check if you can register a trademark against your company name for protection.
- Is the name catchy? Your business name has to resonate with your target audience and to be catchy. To get to that point, it is worth asking for feedback, having a few different names and asking a mixture of family, friends, and trusted business colleagues or mentors for some constructive and honest feedback on your proposals.
- *Make sure you are happy with the name:* It is important to take the time to get the business name right from the start of your entrepreneurial journey. As a business owner, you will have to live with the business name, so make sure you are happy with it, and it resonates with your customers.

In terms of resources, in the early stages, this will depend on the type of business you are planning to start. Some businesses need relatively little in terms of starting up. For example, if you are offering your services as a freelancer in a particular area, you may just need a computer, stationary, and a mobile phone to get begin with.

Some will require considerably more, particularly if you are selling goods: For example, if you are planning to open your own shop, you will need to look at premises and source suppliers and buy stock. In this type of business, a business loan or external funding may be needed.

Another area to think about is whether you need to import particular items, for example, products or parts of products. There will be logistics and regulations to consider, and this can be time consuming. The same logic applies to considering if you need to export any items. This area can range from straightforward to complicated depending on what countries you are planning to import or export from and to and what your home countries trading relationship is with them.

In some cases, you may also need to look at what specialist support you may need for your business. For example, solicitors or patent lawyers may be needed for certain types of business, particularly where you may have to protect an invention from being copied. Another specialist area to consider is accountants. Having accurate and compliant accounts is very important, and it is vital you declare and pay the right amount of taxes. While you always have to consider costs, having the services of a qualified accountant can be less costly than having the tax man chasing you and it may be more time efficient than doing it yourself.

Controlling costs are important through the whole entrepreneurial journey. This is particularly true in the early stages. It is critical to make sure you only spend money on what you really need to get the business started and functioning efficiently. It is important to focus on being practical and prioritizing on what is really needed and not focusing on the superficial. Having what you really need to run the business is much more important than having an expensive city center office or company car to pay for—if you have to prioritize, things like that can come later. Also, at the beginning, there may well be a potential gap (which can vary in length) between starting up and when you will actually start making money; so being pragmatic and practical in the early stages always makes sense.

Depending on what country you are operating from, there may be various types of government support available for new and small business. This can range from anything to start-up loans, support helplines, legal advice, outsourcing public sector work to SMEs, and local and regional business advice. Governments also tend to publish regular reports about the economy's performance. Other relevant information about domestic trade, sector performance, and guidance about importing and exporting to other countries is also likely to be available. This will inevitably vary per country and will also depend on what attitude and approach the government of the day has to business and the economy. However, there will be information and resources available, and it is always worth checking what your business can get in terms of government support.

What Is the Current and Potential Size of the Market?

Whether you are planning to sell goods or services, or both, the current size and potential size of the market are vitally important to the success or failure of the business, particularly at the start-up stages. Ultimately, if there is no demand or potential demand, you may need to rethink your proposition or possibly look at starting a different type of business.

If you have plans for expansion or believe that it is a possibility for the future, having an idea of demand in the future is important. Depending on the industry, this can be a matter of taking an educated guess in some cases.

No matter what the business proposition is not knowing your current and potential market size can ruin your credibility with your peers.

Judging market size is absolutely critical. This will ultimately be helping you judge how much potential business is really out there for your venture. It becomes even more important when attempting to raise external funding for your business, and ultimately, any bank or investor will have to weigh up the market size as part of their assessment of the business and its potential.

When considering market size, it is not only your domestic market that you need to consider. There could also be potential demand for your product in foreign countries. This is where international trade and importing and exporting comes in. An import is something that is brought into your home country from another country. It doesn't matter how it is sent or what the good or service is; if it is produced domestically and sold to another country, the party bringing in the product is the importer, and the import in the receiving country is an export from the sending country.

This can be a massive opportunity if there is demand for your product from other countries; however, there are different logistics, bureaucracy, and regulations to consider when trading with other countries. Areas such as tariff and nontariff barriers need to be considered as well as potential outsourcing and distribution arrangements. Each country will have different levels of regulations, different trading standards for different product types, visa criteria and regulations, exchange rates, differing trade relationships, and "red tape" all of which will have to be factored into your calculations. While trading with other countries may be appealing, it has to be fully planned.

Your home country or the countries you wish to trade with may be members of trading blocs, which are a set of countries that engage in international trade together, usually via a free trade agreement or similar arrangement. Each has various processes, legal obligations, and tariffs, which member states have to abide by.

Examples of trading blocs are the European Union, Mercosur, The Central America Free Trade Area (CAFTA), and The North American Free Trade Area (NAFTA). (Trading blocs are covered in more detail in Chapter 13.)

International trade between countries can vary in terms of cost and complication, but it is another area where if you research thoroughly, you will make an informed choice and a success of how you approach it.

You have to determine market size and value, current, and potential future consumer trends and understand what your competitors have achieved via credible sources. This will result in an informed decision on how to proceed with your business idea.

What Is the Demand for Your Idea?

Once you have an informed idea of the size of your market, another important consideration is the current or potential demand for what your business proposes to offer. Even if there is a large market for the goods or services you are offering, that may not equate to high demand in a mature, saturated, or flooded marketplace.

To calculate this, you will need to look at data on the number of potential customers or number of transactions each year. It is important to look at various reliable sources when looking for this information.

Another area to consider is the volume of sales you need to do to make the business prosper. For example, if you are selling a relatively low-cost item, such as a toothbrush or a pencil, you will need to sell at very large volumes to make the business sustainable. On the other hand, if you are selling high-end cars, you would probably expect to be a lower volume, but because of the higher price, the number of sales needed to achieve sustainability will be lower.

Where Will You Locate Your Business?

Where you locate your business is an important consideration and does depend on the type of business. There are a number of factors to consider when looking at potential locations:

Access for customers: Is the location convenient for your customers to get to?

Staff: Is it the right demographic to get the right type of staff, who you can attract to work for you who are willing to work for the right wage?

Support services: Are there sufficient support services locally or in the vicinity of where you choose?

Cost: A key consideration; having a fancy office in the big city may look good, but the financial cost will be high. Particularly in the early stages, it may be better to have an office in a cheaper location or to work from home if possible. Saving on these costs can be a help, particularly where resources may need to be spread over a number of other areas.

Infrastructure: For example, are there sufficient transport links and accessibility to the location you decide.

Another consideration when deciding on location can be access to and availability of government support. For example, in some countries, governments may offer grants, loans, or tax breaks to business that decides to set up in areas where there is low employment.

Your Working Environment

This is a broad term that refers to all of your surroundings when you are carrying out your working day. This is something that is partly dependent on the type of business and partly dependent on the type of person the entrepreneur may be.

There are a number of different working environments an entrepreneur may find themselves in:

Office: This could be an individual office or could be a "business space" where you can rent a hot desk for whenever you need it.

Work from home: If you have a suitable space, you can use a room in your house and run your business from there. While this offers low cost, convenience, and flexibility, it also has potential drawbacks, such as having too many distractions. Working on your own can be a lonely place in any case but could be magnified by working from home.

Virtual office: This is where you rent a selection of business services that you can use while working from home. In this instance, you are not renting a physical office space. This can include services such as a city center postal address, mail handling services, and video conferencing facilities. This can be suitable if you have stakeholders in different parts of the world, and it is not practical for everyone to meet face-to-face at the regularity needed.

Traveling: For some types of businesses, you may have to travel regularly for face-to-face meetings with clients, suppliers, or other stakeholders.

Each of the aforementioned or a mixture could be viable and comes with its own advantages and disadvantages. It largely depends on what type of business you have, and some working environments go hand in hand with some businesses, whereas with some other businesses, you could have a choice of approaches. Once you are in a position where you know what the options are, you should consider what would suit you personally. We all have different working styles, for example, some people enjoy working alone and some do not. Some individuals will fit certain working environments more than others.

Can Your Idea, Invention, or Product Be Copied?

If you are entering a crowded market, it may be easier for your competitors to copy your idea or do what you are doing.

If you have an invention, have you registered a patent and protected your idea from being copied and produced and ultimately sold as a competitor?

Intellectual property protection stops people copying or stealing:

- Inventions
- The name of your brand and products
- The design and look of your product
- Anything you produce, design, or write

There are a number of protections to consider depending on whether you have a product or service:

- *Patents:* They are used to protect inventions. It gives the right to take legal action against anyone who makes, sells, uses, or imports your invention without your permission. To be granted a patent, your invention has to be new and unique, something that can be made or used and inventive (not something that is a modification of something that already exists). However, patents tend to be expensive, can take a long time to receive due to the research involved, and can be difficult to obtain.
- *Copyright:* It protects your work and stops others from using it without your permission. Copyright protection is automatic in the United Kingdom, and you don't need to apply or pay for it; however, each country's rules in this area vary and the regulations need to be checked.
- *Trademark:* It is registered to protect the brand aspect of your business. An example of this would be the name of the product or service. When you register a trademark, you are able to put a symbol next to your brand to show it belongs to you and therefore warn others against using it.

It is worth getting the relevant legal advice before proceeding here. While this is an important process, it isn't always necessary and can be expensive, so getting the right advice before proceeding at the outset is vital. This is a complex and important area, but protecting your idea and your business is a worthwhile investment.

Do You Know Your Numbers?

In any business, particularly new ones in the early stages, knowing your numbers is nonnegotiable. You have to! If you don't know and fully understand your businesses income and outgoings, their effects, and how they balance, you are going to run into some difficulties, potentially very serious or in some cases irreparable ones. (Understanding Financial Statements is covered in more detail in Chapter 9.)

In simple terms, your business needs to be making more than it spends. While that sounds obvious, it is not a given that this will always happen particularly in the short term or if your business is seasonal. In some cases, it may be a while before you are making regular profits. Outgoings have to be sensibly estimated and calculated as well as the potential income that you plan to generate. This will then show what that means for your turnover and how it translates to profit and loss.

Knowing your numbers is also vital in terms of credibility. When discussing your business, be it with peers at a networking event, potential investors, or even friends and family, knowing and understanding where your business stands financially can make or break your credibility as a business person. This in itself can have an effect on your personal brand and the likelihood of fellow business people choosing to work with and/or invest in you.

In terms of approach, a good "rule of thumb," particularly in the early stages, may be to overestimate your costs and underestimate your income and expect the unexpected. That is not a defeatist approach; it's more pragmatic and realistic. It allows for any unforeseen costs that may come up. Balancing that with a sensible approach to calculating income means you will have realistic expectations and in turn a healthy balance sheet.

How Strong Is Your Network?

A popular phrase in business and in life is "it's not what you know, it's who you know." This is true to some extent and can be helpful at all stages of the entrepreneurial journey.

If you know people who can help promote your business or if you know an experienced business person who could potentially be a business mentor, this can be particularly advantageous if you are in the early stages or very new to running your own business.

However, that is not to say that you cannot build a strong and effective network from scratch. You have to start somewhere, there are many business networking events to attend, many different groups to join, and there is also the power of social media. If used effectively, a mixture or all of these can be used to build a strong network. This is covered in more detail in Chapter 7.

Will the Life of an Entrepreneur Suit You?

Broadly speaking, the entrepreneurial lifestyle is unpredictable and does not offer the predictability or security of set hours or of a guaranteed salary at the end of each month. So, there may be a need to sacrifice or compromise, as it is unlikely you will be doing "Monday to Friday, 9 a.m. to 5 p.m." This can be particularly magnified when getting a business established and can stabilize in the time thereafter. Having a business that is yours and your responsibility will mean that you will rarely be able to switch off from it and that can be a mixture of exhilarating, exciting, and sometimes frustrating, all at the same time. It can also be a reality that you have to run your new business in addition to your day job while you are getting setup and established. This may be a necessity if you have fixed financial commitments and need a certain to generate amount of income (that your new business may not achieve straight away).

It also tends to mean that you may have to do everything to keep all of the business operations on track. Things can unexpectedly go wrong, and if you are a start-up or a small business, the likelihood is that, as is likely you are the only employee, you will have to fix it. If you have expanded, you may have employees who can take some of the responsibility, but the ultimate responsibility lies at the top.

Cash flow is another challenge for any business. Cash flow challenges can be caused by anything; from late invoicing by the business to late receiving of payment by customers or clients. This can lead to a potential "domino effect" where one delay can cause multiple delays in payments. This can lead to difficulty in paying yourself, your suppliers, and your bills. While steps can be taken to mitigate these problems, this is a very real consideration to make when deciding to start your own business and vastly different from a secure monthly salary that comes with most full-time employment.

The entrepreneurial lifestyle, with all of its potentially massive advantages and the inevitability of some challenges, is a big consideration in any case, no matter what business you are starting, working toward expanding, or have established. The effects can be magnified when entering a volatile market or introducing a completely new product or concept.

How Will the Business Affect You and Your Family?

The potentially long and unpredictable hours and potential unpredictability of income is a key consideration, particularly if you have a family who depends on you.

While being an entrepreneur can deliver big rewards, the time and attention that any business needs at all stages is considerable.

Being an entrepreneur isn't always what you think.

Entrepreneurship has undoubtedly become more mainstream, and to some extent, the perception has arguably also shifted. For every successful millionaire, there will be start-ups that are struggling to establish themselves for various reasons. It is often said that "over half of new businesses fail"—a statement that is probably an over simplistic and over generalized. According to various sources, around 80 percent of businesses survive the first year, but when it gets to the five-year mark, between 45 and 50 percent fail at that point.

So, some ventures do not work and there are reasons, and some of which can be mitigated.

For example, some businesses fail due to:

- *Lack of market research:* Not fully understanding your market, your competitors, and the potential demand for the products or services that you offer.
- *Lack of a solid business plan:* Planning is important and gives a template to work against. Not giving enough thought or consideration to the key parts of the business, plan can lead to unforeseen problems.
- *Financial shortfall and poor pricing:* Not having the necessary funding to keep the business running or setting a price that is too low or too high.
- *Poor choice of location:* This is particularly important if you are setting up a retail business. You would want to have a location which has high footfall, attracts customers, and does not have too many similar businesses in the surrounding area.
- *Poor marketing:* Not having a targeted and relevant marketing plan will ultimately mean that the chances of people finding out about your business and what it can provide are considerably lower.
- *Rigidity:* The business world is constantly changing and the level or severity of that change varies in different countries and different industries. What is important is that any

business is in a position to adapt to change and "move with the times" as quickly and efficiently as possible.

- *Growing too quickly:* As your business gets established and you make progress, the opportunity for growth goes from being something thought about to an exciting opportunity. However, there are risks to growing too quickly, and if your business is not fully prepared for growth, it can cause challenges.

When starting a business, there will be times that you will have to keep the faith and times where you will have to adapt. It is not always easy.

At times, there may be a divide between what you want to do and what you have to do. As an entrepreneur, there are multiple "plates to spin." That means taking responsibility and having to make tough calls.

Making a Decision

A SWOT analysis is a useful tool that could be used throughout the entrepreneurial journey. It can provide an entrepreneur with a perspective on what a business can do well, where any potential problems lie, and which opportunities to pursue. A personal SWOT analysis can do the same for an individual.

The acronym stands for:

- **S**trengths: Any characteristics of the business or individual that give an advantage over others.
  Examples of business strength could be high standard of process management, top-quality employees, or proven customer loyalty.
  Examples of an individual's strengths could be previous business experience and expertise, marketing or creative skills, and negotiation skills.
- **W**eaknesses: Any characteristics of the business or individual that give a disadvantage relative to others.
  Examples of business weakness could be lack of resources, lack of available funding, or inefficient processes.
  Examples of an individual's weaknesses could be lack of mental toughness or poor listening skills.

- **O**pportunities: Any elements in the external environment that a business or individual could use to its advantage.
  Examples of business opportunities could be potential to access new or emerging markets, looking to work with local government, or to embrace the opportunities of new technology.
  Examples of an individual's opportunities could be opportunities for networking and a potential to learn new skills.
- **T**hreats: Any elements in the external environment that could cause difficulty for the business or individual.
  Examples of business threats could be increased competition domestically and abroad, the need for greater levels of compliance, and increased levels of government bureaucracy.
  Examples of an individual's threats could be economic uncertainty or rival products that are already in your marketplace.

When using a SWOT, it is important to recognize:

- That all four categories interrelate.
- The need to prioritize, probably in terms of likely relative impact, the factors identified in each quadrant.
- All four categories need to be populated and always applied, no exceptions.
- Because this framework is a snapshot and all businesses operate in an environment of relentless change, there is a need to regularly review and update the key issues placed in each quadrant.

A typical SWOT diagram could look like this:

Strengths	Weaknesses
Opportunities	Threats

If you decide to use SWOT to help with the decision-making process, the most important thing is to ensure that you are being honest. It completely defeats the object if you are not up front about each category.

While you strive for success, you also have to be prepared for failure. Things don't always run smoothly or to plan, and unfortunately, in some cases, not all businesses work. There will be some failure at some point, minor, large, or something in between. An entrepreneur will typically fail fast, fix fast, and learn from it.

The reality is that the risk of failure is ever present and daunting when you are leading the business, but if you accept that, recover from it, and learn from it, it will keep stay on the right path and continue to strive for and achieve success.

The biggest risk is not taking any risk.
—Mark Zuckerberg

CHAPTER 3

How Can You Grow Your Business?

Without continual growth and progress, such words as improvement, and success have no meaning.

—Benjamin Franklin

Growing a business is undoubtedly an exciting part of the entrepreneurial adventure. A business that has solid foundations, is being well received by customers and is making a profit is in a great position to grow. Getting to that position is a big achievement.

Even if in the early stages the expanding isn't a key priority, it is important to give your business the best chance of thriving, because if it is thriving it has the best opportunity to stay successful and gives the best foundation for growth.

To have a thriving business, you should always look at the following principles:

1. Get to know and understand what your customers want. Ultimately, your business will be looking to provide a product or service that solves a customer's problem. You can gain important insight from your customers by offering a personalized service and asking for feedback.

2. Offer great customer service. Exceptional customer service and going the extra mile is vital to retain customers, to get referrals, and to attract new customers. Making the customer service journey smooth and pleasant will be remembered (equally a poor customer service will also not be forgotten).

3. Always look for new customers (but don't forget your existing ones!). Attracting new customers is important, and this can be

done via special offers or some sort of price reduction. However, it is important to balance this with looking after your long-standing customers.

4. Look at and measure what works and adapt where necessary. It is worthwhile to review progress at set intervals and measure progress. This is a time where the business plan can be referred back to for clarification. Whether you are ahead of your plan, a bit behind, or on track, if you need to adapt your ways of working to improve, then do so. If a certain of your business can be improved, then in any case it is best to do that at the earliest opportunity.

There are a number of different definitions of business growth. This gives an insight into how a business can grow.

- *Organic growth:* This is the most common (and some may say effective) means of growing a business. This type of growth needs a business to focus on producing more products and services for success. A focus on organic growth may mean a business will acquire more space, for example, a larger office or expanding shifts to produce more product. A business that is growing organically literally needs to expand to cope with increased demand. This is a solid growth strategy for new businesses and for a business that is new to the market and faces a shortage in product.
- *Strategic business growth:* This is a longer term growth strategy that follows on when the potential for organic growth has reached its limit. A strategic growth approach may be to reach a previously untapped market through a new product or through increased advertising. This growth strategy requires money that can be generated through organic growth and strategic growth that will be achieved by a gradual increase in sales. This strategy allows a business to focus on long-term growth goals and use saved or stored capital to achieve this objective.
- *Partnership/acquisition/merger:* Some types of business can be suitable for this type of growth. It can produce some unique

benefits and opportunities for expansion. However, this is one of the riskier paths to growth despite offering a lot of potential success. A well-planned merger or acquisition can open doors to new markets, help to manufacture more products, broaden skills and expertise within the business, and gain customer loyalty that has been cultivated from the other brand. However, this type of arrangement can lead to complications; two separate entities coming together are not always straightforward and wherever possible any issues should be ironed out before signing any agreement.

- *Rapid business growth:* This type of business growth occurs when growth is needed in a short period of time and rapid growth is the only option. A prospect for rapid growth could arise due to an unexpected opportunity. This usually means a rapid increase in production and/or staffing levels, and this will lead to certain challenges and risks. Customer service issues, operational efficiency issues, outgrowing premises, and shortfalls in cash flow can occur with this type of business growth. As the growth rate increases, your cash will go out of the business and costs will increase as well, and if this happens too quickly, this can spiral out of control and the financial solvency of the business could be put at risk.

Timing is important when deciding to go ahead with expansion, and there are some criteria to hit before making considering and making the decision to expand. These indicators will show whether you are at the best point to consider growth:

1. *Having regular customers:* A positive flow of customers is very important. Before deciding to expand, you definitely want to have a steady (ideally increasing) flow of customers. Repeat customers also give your business stability. All of these factors show that there is continued demand for your product or service.
2. *There is customer demand for growth:* If your customers are asking more of your product or service, or increased opening hours, then that is a good gauge to look at expansion.

3. *You have a positive balance sheet and regular profits:* If this is the case and is showing over a relatively long period of time (or at the very least heading in the right direction), this shows that you have a healthy balance sheet and that your business could be ready for growth.

4. *Your industry is growing:* It tends to be easier to grow your business if you are in an industry that is growing. Similarly, you may want to think again if your industry is standing still or shrinking. (It is not impossible to grow in these circumstances, but there is likely to be more pitfalls in a stagnant or shrinking market.)

5. *Your current business cannot handle the demand (or is getting close to that point):* If you are in this position, then there is sufficient demand for thinking about getting larger premises, opening new premises, or taking on extra staff.

These criteria are each very important, and all need to be considered before deciding to go ahead with growth. You need to ensure that your business is ready to grow. If you go too soon, the business may not survive. If possible, it is worth waiting to ensure you are ready as this minimizes risk. If you are patient and go for it at the right time, you will maximize your chances of growing successfully.

When you feel you have considered and met the criteria for growth and you are thinking you and your business is ready, then growth can be a feasible and exciting option.

However, growing a business can be daunting, particularly if it is new to you. If your business plan includes a plan for growth, then it is worth referring back to it at this stage. However, if growth was not part of the original plan, it can be updated and your plan for growth can be added in. Either way, having this to refer back to and to measure progress, will be helpful.

How you expand will to some extent depend on circumstances, and some business models can be more straightforward to expand than others. But having a plan is vital as there are many things that can potentially go wrong.

To successfully grow your business, then the following broad principles should be considered:

1. *Retain and recapture existing customers:* While attracting new customers is always likely to be beneficial and is never a bad approach, it isn't the only way to grow. In some cases, the retention and recapture of current customers is the best bet for increasing sales. Customers who have bought a product or used a service once are likely to do so again if they have a positive customer experience. Marketing and data capture of shopping habits is important here and can be used to convert one time customers into repeat customers.

2. *Actively ask for referrals:* You can't just assume that customers are spreading the word about your business. (They may well be, but an assumption is hard to measure and plan against.) Your current customers are already in your target market, so it is fair to suggest that their work and/or social circles are also part of your target market. Depending on the type and size of your business, you can incentivize referrals with a discount code or ask customers to tag or share your brand on social media channels.

3. *Manage, monitor, and contain your costs carefully:* When expanding, it is vital to keep an eye on costs. Ultimately, if your business expands and your costs increase too much, then this can lead to not having enough money left to invest to make a profit. So, when you are looking at growing, pay attention to how much it costs to run the business and how much it costs to deliver products or services to customers. You can cut costs by removing low-performing products or services and by improving marketing to improve inventory turnover. However, there is a balance to be struck here. While costs always need to be managed, don't cut costs in a way that will detrimentally impact your employees or customers. That may lead to increased cash flow in the short term, but in the medium and long term, it is likely to damage your business and as a result its potential to grow.

4. *Expand and extend your market reach:* There are many ways of doing this depending on the type of business. For example, open new premises in different locations or have an online shop, targeting a new demographic via market research and social media and by showcasing new uses and benefits of your product or service. Any and all of these approaches will help increase market share. This will lead to increased sales and stabilize the business model. In any case, having

more than one type of customer is beneficial as it will make your business more resilient to market changes.

5. *Network:* There are many different available options to network in an effective way, via events and social media (this is covered in more detail in Chapter 7), and is another way to build positive relationships, meet new people and "spread the word" about your business. Networking can lead to new customers and clients as well as useful relationships with other business owners who may be able to help your business in some way. This can open doors to new opportunities, new markets, and opportunities to collaborate.

6. *Be diverse with your products or services:* Broadly speaking, this can be done in two ways. Firstly, by focusing on the products or services that you already sell that address the needs of the customers you already have. Or secondly, by focusing on new markets that have similar needs and characteristics to those of your current customers. Both approaches can be done in a gradual way allowing for diversification of products and reaching new customers without overextending the business.

7. *Consider exporting to international markets (this is covered in more detail in Chapter 13):* This approach means reaching a potentially large number of customers in diverse geographic locations outside of the domestic market. However, this approach will always need a lot of time and resources. This can be complex as different countries have different trading laws and regulations. There may also be additional licenses that are needed to trade between certain countries as well as various regulations regarding different products, as well as the possibility of additional paperwork such as work permits. If you have the time and resources, there is no doubt that exporting will give access to previously inaccessible markets and that will create huge opportunities for growth.

It is key to choose the right growth strategy that will suit your business. Every business is unique and will be at different stages of development and that will be key to any decision that needs to be made. Not all growth strategies will suit every business or appeal to every business owner.

While any strategy will not necessarily lead to growth straight away, if the plan is implemented consistently and systematically, there will be positive progress. And if that strategy doesn't work for whatever reason, be prepared to step back, honestly analyze what the issues were, and make a new plan to go again.

Growth cannot come by taking the easy way.
—Paul V. Johnson

CHAPTER 4

Stakeholders

The best way to minimize disagreement is to ensure that all stakeholders are in the room.

—Cheryl Yeoh

Stakeholder management is a key activity at all junctures for any business. It is a critical process for all business activity that must be well thought out, continually planned for, and adaptable to change. Keeping every stakeholder happy, despite potentially having different priorities, objectives, and expectations, is vitally important; can be difficult and can at times, be thankless. However, there is no way around it, and it has to be done and is an important part of ensuring your business has the best possible foundation for success.

The first step is to identify who your stakeholders are or are likely to be. A stakeholder is anyone who has an interest in the success or failure of the business, anyone with power and influence over the business, and anyone who may be directly or sometimes perceive themselves to be affected by work or activities carried out by the business. Stakeholders can be organizations, groups of people, or individuals and can be managed upward, downward, or sideways. If your stakeholder is an organization, make sure you identify the right person/people to communicate with, within that organization.

Generically speaking, stakeholder management comprises of:

- Identifying, recognizing, and acknowledging different stakeholders and their individual or common interests
- Determining their level of influence, while recognizing that it can change
- Establishing a robust communication plan for all stakeholders
- Influencing and engaging stakeholders

There are a number of key stakeholders to consider when starting, running, and expanding your own business, and they can be split into internal and external stakeholders.

Internal Stakeholders

Any individual or group who contributes to the businesses internal functions or is directly affected by management decisions can be considered as an internal stakeholder. The management of internal stakeholders involves ensuring they enjoy the company culture, are engaged in company goals, and feel like they are an important part of the team.

The following are the examples of internal stakeholders.

Owners/shareholders: They are liable for the impact the business has and also take a significant role in strategy. They are likely to take the majority (or all) of the key decisions regarding internal and external stakeholders. Owners are interested in the business performance, the balance sheet, and the resulting profit or loss.

Managers: They have a significant role in the business operational decisions, are accountable for decision making, and are the link between the owners/shareholders and the employees. Managers are concerned with employee performance in the business area they are responsible for and salary.

Employees: They have significant time and financial investment in the business. They want job security and a good salary or reward scheme for their work. They are also interested in being and feeling valued for their contribution, and as such, a well-run business will take into account employee values, concerns, and opinions and use that insight to help shape the business strategy.

External Stakeholders

Anyone who is outside the business and not involved in the internal functions but has an interest in its operation, performance, and well-being can be an external stakeholder. Management of external stakeholders is a team effort where each part of the business may deal with different stakeholders.

The following are the examples of external stakeholders.

Suppliers: This is an interdependent relationship where the success of one business will impact the success of another. A strong relationship with suppliers is key. Suppliers will want the business to buy supplies from them and potentially create a long-term, mutually beneficial business relationship, with timely payments, shipments, and robust and effective processes.

Customers: Understanding the core needs of customers is significant part of running a prosperous business. Interacting with customers, who want the business to produce high-quality goods or services and sell at a reasonable price, is an important part of understanding and delivering their needs.

Banks: They may have provided start-up capital or some sort of loan and will want the business to be well run and successful. They will also expect to be kept updated with progress, so they can be confident that they have a secure investment and ultimately get repaid.

Lenders: People (other than banks) who could have lent the business money, again will want the business to be run effectively and successfully, and who want any money they have loaned to be paid back on time and within agreed timescales.

Investors: They will take a keen interest in the business, all areas of the balance sheet, and how it is running, and, in some cases, they may play a big part in the day-to-day operations. Investors want a return on any money they have invested.

Government: It has an interest in business that is contributing to the economy and productivity, making tax contributions, spending money, and employing people. A government also sets regulations, with regard to accounting, employment, and ethical and legal concerns, and looks to ensure that businesses are handling and managing these responsibilities in an ethical and appropriate way.

Local community: There can be many effects a business can have on a community. They have an interest as the business may employ local people, have community development programs, and give access to unique goods or services. However, there can be negative effects such as increased traffic volume, increased pollution, and poor business practices and effects on other businesses in the area. So, community engagement needs to be maximized and any negative repercussions minimized.

Society: As the business world has changed and evolved, particularly with the digital and global economy, businesses can have an effect on society as a whole. Fast food outlets raise debate about health; social media companies raise debate about influencing, safeguarding, and data sharing; and some other industries have transformed over time. These changes are not all good or all bad and can be debated; however, the business as a whole has a responsibility to ensure that the overall outcome of their activities is as positive for society as possible.

Once you have understood who your key stakeholders are and their priorities, you are then in a position to develop strategies to influence them. It is also worth noting that as your business evolves or grows, your stakeholders can change. This is something to keep under regular review. Key areas to consider are as follows:

- What are the key motivators of your stakeholders?
- What information do they need from you and how regularly do they want it?
- What emotional or financial interest do they have in your work and is it positive or negative?
- Who and what influences their opinions and their opinions of you?
- Are there conflicting interests among your stakeholders?
- What powers do your stakeholders have and what influences can they exert?

All of these stakeholders can also be grouped as per what level of interest they have in the business and the power they have over it. This is sometimes referred to as stakeholder prioritization. Depending on what type of business you have, there could potentially be a long list of people and organizations that are affected by it. Some of these people may be able to help advance your business or block progress.

There are a number of tools and studies that look at stakeholder management. A good and simple way to prioritize is to use Mendelow's stakeholder matrix and to look at each stakeholders' power and interest and then group and prioritize from there. For example, a fellow director would have high power and interest in the business projects. Family may have high interest in your business but (if they are not owners/shareholders/employees) are unlikely to have power over it. So, in a nutshell:

High power and low interest Would need to be kept on side and satisfied, but not so engaged that they become bored or frustrated with your message	*High interest and high power* These people are key players and would be top priority and are the people who will need most engagements and go to every effort to satisfy
Low interest and low power Least important and minimum effort: This group would need monitoring, but not regular communication	*Low power and high interest* Would need to be communicated with regularly and ensure that no major problems come up

This is just to name a few areas to consider, but this shows that there is a lot to think about when it comes to understanding your key stakeholders.

In terms of managing stakeholder relationships, there are several key principles to consider:

- *Understanding what success means for everyone:* This is key and can be very complex, particularly if, as is sometimes the case, there are differing definitions of success between different stakeholders and how success could be achieved. This is where the art of negotiation and recognizing, understanding, and appreciating different interests becomes important.
- *Consult early and regularly:* Answering key questions and getting information and ideas early can avoid complications at a later stage and, in some cases, avoid unwanted or unexpected surprises.
- *Communication and ensuring that there are communication systems in place to meet the requirements of all stakeholders:*

Ultimately, it is necessary to keep all stakeholders "in the loop"; when managing varying interests, having different interests is almost inevitable and not communicating properly can unnecessarily magnify issues. It is important to ensure that the intended message is clear and understood with the intention of getting the desired, positive response.

- *The art of compromise:* This can be important, particularly when you are in the position of opposite or conflicting interests or definitions of success. Ultimately, one or more parties may have to compromise for the bigger picture success.

- *Taking responsibility:* As in any aspect of running your own business, being willing and able to front up and take responsibility is not only necessary but also helps to create credibility in you as a businessperson.

- *Even though it's not always easy, try and keep it simple:* Show that you care. Listening to your stakeholders and being understanding and empathetic to concerns can make all the difference.

- *Consultation and remembering we are all human:* Being aware and mindful of other people's feelings is vital when dealing with different stakeholders. In a lot of cases, people aren't deliberately trying to be difficult; this is where listening, empathy, and compromise again become essential.

Understand stakeholder symmetry: Find the appropriate balance of competing claims by various groups of stakeholders.

—Warren G. Bennis

CHAPTER 5

Uncertainty, Risk, and Change

Adapt and change before any major trends or changes.

—Jack Ma

Your business will be created in an environment of change, the new (or not so new) normal. Our working lives are generally underpinned by uncertainty, instability, and sometimes volatility.

This naturally means that the dynamics of your business will be constantly changing. In some cases, the triggers for change will be from within your business (the internal environment) and in other times from the outside (the external environment). There will be times when change will be caused by a combination of internal and external factors.

In general terms, the rate of change is increasing, and business owners must embrace this reality. An example could be working hours. As entrepreneurs, and in increasing cases the working world, the expectation of us working 9 a.m. to 5 p.m. Monday to Friday is an increasingly rare reality. There needs to be a degree of flexibility, to work those hours necessary to take the business forward while achieving your chosen work–life balance.

Depending on what products or services your business offers, there needs to be a recognition of the significance and potential of technology and artificial intelligence (AI). As a minimum, it is likely, for example, that all entrepreneurs need to embrace the potential of social media.

Types of Change

There are several different types of change. However, in most cases, there are two main categories to understand and recognize.

Transactional change: This type of change might refer to changes in your business processes. This is where your key processes will continually evolve to meet any changing requirements. This type of change is usually planned and systematic, where you change a process toward an identified outcome.

Examples may include altering the way you invoice or process and accept payments, changing your supply chain, or evolving your planning processes.

Transformational change: This type of change will include every aspect of your business and will be enacted over a (usually short) period of time. As entrepreneurs, this could mean a restructure, a change in your product or service offering, deciding to outsource certain aspects of your business, or possibly a change in direction or overall strategy.

Your role in this type of change is pivotal. You need to ensure every aspect of your business is actively and meaningfully involved. In the early stages, this may be just you, and in later stages, it could involve employees, contactors, or other outsource partners, all of whom could be affected by changes you make. Any proposed changes need to be viable, be clear, and be inspirational to those around you.

The Complexities of Change

The reality is, that ongoing and continuous change is inevitable—something to be accepted by all of us.

If we fail to, or perhaps even choose not to move with the times, there may be consequences. In terms of your business, this may mean harmful and permanent consequences. So, an entrepreneur needs to have a successful, adaptable, and sustainable change management strategy to give the optimum chance of surviving and thriving in an ever more competitive arena.

There will undeniably be occasions when you need to have the courage to challenge and critically analyze the way you do things. An example of this could be deciding to change as a result of an unexpected problem or changing processes to prepare your business for growth. Internal and/

or external change must be successfully accommodated and is therefore an absolute priority.

We need also to remember that there is both planned and unplanned change. Preparations for planned change can and should be made in advance as much as is reasonably possible. This gives the concurrent opportunity for you to have detailed, realistic, and sustainable implementation strategies. However, reality tells us that not all changes can be reasonably planned for or anticipated. The impact of unplanned change can be instant, destabilizing and extremely disruptive. However, this still needs to be prepared for or mitigated in the most effective possible way. It is essential to have a robust contingency plan in place to try and neutralize the impacts of any unexpected change. Examples of unplanned change could include sudden large-scale system outages, an unexpected severe economic downturn, or a political change that negatively affects the business community.

The External Environment

Understanding the context within which your business operates is critically important. By having a current (then very regularly updated) knowledge and awareness of the external environment will give you the opportunity to be more effective in accommodating change and calculating and managing risk.

A brief explanation as to why this is so important. The principle of the significance of the external environment to your business is based on Systems Theory (1937). The implications for you and your business are as follows:

- That your business is an open-looped system that is dependent on and interrelated to the external environment as a prerequisite for your longer term survival.
- Therefore, your internal business environment and external environments are inevitably interrelated. By way of clarity and inevitability, both environments are constantly changing!

The categories of external change that you need to identify and understand in terms of your business can be placed in a PESTLE framework. This framework is a snapshot (i.e., at that moment in time, so can become quickly outdated) of the six following categories:

P = Political
E = Economic
S = Social
T = Technological
L = Legal
E = Environmental

You may find it helpful to create your own PESTLE framework so that you have a dynamic, regularly reviewed and updated awareness of these business-critical external factors.

Always remember:

- That all six categories apply, always with no exceptions.
- At a moment in time, one or more of the six categories may have a greater significance for your business.
- The six categories are inevitably interrelated, so a single external factor may appear in more than one category, albeit in a different context.
- You need to constantly prioritize and reprioritize these external factors in terms of their known or expected impacts on your business.

Examples From the PESTLE Framework That Will Impact Your Business

Political

- The current central and local government policies
- An impending election and political public opinion
- The political benefits of a government (some may be more pro-business and pro-trade than others)

Economic

- The level of relative prosperity or economic recession
- The rate of inflation
- Levels of unemployment
- The rate of economic growth domestically and abroad
- Levels of direct and indirect taxation
- Levels of business and consumer confidence
- The impacts of fluctuating exchange rates

Social

- Demographic trends
- Age distribution
- Influence of the mainstream and local media
- The impact of social media
- External perceptions of your business's brand and values
- Usual and changing lifestyles and habits
- Evolving consumer attitudes, tastes, and values
- Ethical perspectives

Technological

- The rate of change and technological innovation
- The trend toward automation
- Awareness of competitor strategies
- The evolving and increasing range of technological communication and delivery channels

Legal

- Employee and workers' rights
- Consumer protection
- Discrimination laws
- Equal opportunities
- Health and safety
- Legislation to encourage or restrict competition
- Tax regulations

Environmental

- Environmental laws and regulations
- The swing toward reducing the carbon footprint across the world
- Sustainability
- Various pressure groups
- Increasing stakeholder awareness of the importance of protecting the environment

An alternative framework you may find useful in this context is a SWOT analysis (this is also covered in Chapter 2).

Here, you can look to pinpoint and understand the key internal strengths and weaknesses and also external opportunities and threats that may impact your business at any one point in time. As with the PESTLE discussed earlier, you therefore have a greater opportunity to manage and mitigate risk and accommodate change.

Some key factors that may apply to your business:

Strengths:

- High-quality employees
- Effective business leadership and management
- The quality and reliability of your processes
- Your business producing high-quality products or services
- Establishing a strong unique selling point (USP)

Weaknesses:

- Limited capacity or resources
- Shortage of space
- Lack of financial support or funding
- Poor reputation
- Poor management of costs and overheads
- Inefficient processes

Opportunities:

- Looking to build and expand your market share
- Developing an influential marketing strategy

- Having a strong brand
- Robust social media strategy

Threats:

- Competition: Both new and current
- Cost fluctuations in supply chains
- Poor or minimal consumer awareness of your offerings
- Over reliance on specific suppliers

Technology and AI

The influence of technology and AI is constantly evolving and will inevitably increase over time.

As an entrepreneur, aspects of these relentless changes you need to consider include the following:

- The benefits of having a website.
- Your presence, activity, and profile on social media.
- The cost, resource, and opportunity cost implications: In addition to your people and premises, technology and AI are most likely to be a very significant overhead.

Your Role in Leading Change

There are several key roles an entrepreneur will need to adopt when leading change. We could well argue that as change is the norm, as a result demonstrating these roles is "business as usual":

- Being a role model: This is where you lead by example. Where you react appropriately, sensibly, and proportionately to change and guide and lead those around you, both inside and outside of your business, through change.
- Having a clear vision and strategy: When navigating through change, it becomes critical that you have a clear plan and strategy to deal with it. A visible, succinct, and well-communicated strategy will enable awareness, understanding, and application for all your stakeholders, including you.

- Inspiring others: You are the fulcrum of inspiration for all those around you. If your key stakeholders trust and believe in you, you are motivated by you then any change adventure may well be more acceptable and coherent.

- Having a clear communication strategy: Before, during, and in some cases after any change, you must have a clear communication strategy. For many of your stakeholders, maybe even for you, change can be daunting and unsettling. Any stakeholder reactions to change can be accompanied by elements of doubt or even lack of trust in you as entrepreneur if they are not sure what is going on. You need to have a clear, honest, and transparent communications strategy, using any and all appropriate communication channels, so that all your stakeholders are kept fully and regularly informed. This applies whether the change is welcome, for example, a new product launch, or when news of change is not so welcome, for example, a delay in distribution.

- Stakeholder management: Mendelow's matrix is discussed in detail elsewhere in detail in Chapter 4 and emphasizes the need for you to understand and accommodate all your key internal/external stakeholder priorities and expectations. Your stakeholder's agendas can and will differ, in some cases, dramatically. Your role as entrepreneur is to meet or exceed your stakeholder expectations by adopting the right balance. Your optimum stakeholder balance will also constantly change.

- Emotional intelligence: You need to understand and manage your own reactions to change. You also need to be aware of, respect, and understand the emotions and reactions of the various key stakeholders. You therefore look to balance and accommodate your own feelings and those of others as you navigate through ongoing change. As an entrepreneur, there may be times when you may decide to pause and reflect before taking any action. Throughout you must make every effort to demonstrate empathy and understanding.

Essential Skills and Competencies During Change

As an entrepreneur, there are a range of skills and competencies that are likely become even more important during times of uncertainty and change. These include the following:

- Building collaborative relationships: There is a need for you to develop and sustain key stakeholder relationships. Each stakeholder, whether internal or external, will require an individual approach, with mutual awareness, respect, and understanding being fundamental aspects throughout.

- Continuous personal development: As an entrepreneur, you must constantly embrace learning, experiences, and knowledge. This allows for continual development. In any regularly changing environment, nothing stands still. Therefore, you and those around you or working with you must look to embrace the philosophy of lifelong learning. Ideally you and your employees should have a development plan which gives you a framework to support your professional, entrepreneurial lives, and lives outside of work. If your workplace encourages learning, acquisition of knowledge, and personal development, there is a greater chance of effectively and successfully navigating through change.

- Listening skills: Many view this as an extremely high-level skill; however, this is crucial for you as an entrepreneur. Amidst the realities of day-to-day business life, when in contact with others, allowing them to convey their message, viewpoint, or feelings while saying nothing in response and also being 100 percent attentive can be challenging in some cases. However, this is exactly what you need to do when you are looking to productively engage with your stakeholders and take them with you through change.

- Self-motivation: Through change, you need to demonstrate a relentless desire and appetite for achieving the desired outcome. Everyone around you, your key stakeholders, will be looking to you for inspiration and encouragement through

change, especially if and when any difficulties are encoun-
tered. As an entrepreneur, you need to actively demonstrate
a drive and energy to maintain the momentum of change.
Outwardly, you never hint at giving up and others will feed
off your positivity.

- Self-reflection: This is another lifelong skill. This is very
closely aligned with your continuous professional and personal development. This skill implies ongoing self-challenge.
Where we regularly take the time to pause and reflect on what
has happened and consider what can and has been learnt. This
means your business can benefit from any lessons learned next
time. Without doubt, if you and any employees actively apply
this philosophy, then as a result your ability to cope with and
deliver change is considerably enhanced.

- Verbal and nonverbal communication: As an entrepreneur,
you will often be in the spotlight. Others will scrutinize what
you say, when, where, and how. This is the case even more so
during times of change. Your tone of voice, clarity of message, eye contact, honesty, credibility, integrity, and being
self-awareness are some of the many aspects to consider. You
will also need to be adaptable, demonstrating this range of
complex skills in a unique way for each stakeholder.

Individual and Collective Reactions to Change

Every one of us reacts differently to change. It is therefore vital that you
understand your personal response to change and the response of those
around you.

Some of the variables you need to consider include the following:

- The job security of your employees could be at risk during
times of change.
- The sway of some your employees: Collectively, they will
influence each other. In some cases, it only needs one negative
influence to start with.
- The need for your employees to feel valued, where their contributions are recognized.

- How you involve your employees, giving them a meaningful role to take throughout change.
- How you keep your employees informed: A clear communication plan is needed.
- How far your workplace culture embraces change, creativity, innovation, and ideas.
- The level of mutual trust and respect: This aspect can make a significant difference to how change is accepted and embraced.

Your Choices With Change

How you, as entrepreneur, respond to change depends on several key factors:

- The change itself and its implications, now and in the short, medium, and long term
- The timing of the change
- Previous experience of change and of managing change
- Internal and external stakeholder views and influence
- The reactions of family and friends

This clearly implies that the way each of us sees change, while being unique, is influenced by a range of interrelated business and nonbusiness factors that in themselves will constantly change.

We live in an imperfect world, so when you respond to change, the priority is to make the right choice or the best choice available at the time. Ensure you have awareness of your viable options and get as much information as you can. If possible, seek the advice, expertise, and opinions of others who may have knowledge of what choices you are facing. Making as informed decision as possible is always preferable.

Whenever possible, know that your decision is the best that it can possibly be at that moment in time.

If you focus on results, you will never change. If you focus on change, you will get results.

—Jack Dixon

CHAPTER 6

Short-, Medium-, and Long-Term Planning

He who fails to plan is planning to fail.

—Winston Churchill

It is often said that "proper planning prevents poor performance." This is certainly true in business and is probably true in life as well!

Starting, running, and expanding your own business can be a mixture of exciting, daunting, and challenging. There are numerous areas to think about and manage, some of which may be completely new territory. This is where planning comes in very useful. Not only will this break down what you are trying to achieve, but it will also give vital structure to work to and milestones to measure progress. There is a price for nonexistent or poor planning. This can be wasted time, missed deadline, and wasted effort as well as financial costs, such as losing control of budgets. Having a clear and robust planning process will undoubtedly be a big help and give your business a solid structure to work to.

Business planning will outline all of the strategies and actions you will take to ensure your business is prosperous, survives, and has a sound foundation for future growth and beyond. Good planning will lead to good management of each of the areas of your business.

Every new business needs a business plan. This acts as a blueprint of how you will start and develop your new business, backed up by detailed and high-quality research. A business plan is a vital document in so many ways and isn't something just to create and then put away and never look at again. As previously mentioned, this is a document that you will refer back to as your business develops and grows. It will certainly be needed if you wish to attract external investment, as any investor will be highly unlikely to invest without (among other things) a solid, well-thought-out, business plan, showing how you see your business progressing and delivering in the future.

Planning is a big part of the ongoing process, from the start-up phase through to day-to-day operations and planning for expansion. This will encompass all of the planning needed to run a successful business as well as scoping out the competition and how your business will fit into the market and industry. The process of reviewing progress should be done at regular intervals in addition to setting new goals as current goals are achieved.

There are three key steps that can be used to help with the general business planning process:

1. Create a plan. This is where the business owner can start, by establishing and recording key details. Being clear and concise is key here, but ultimately it needs to have substance as well. This means you can refer back to it as the business takes shape and you can compare the plan to the actual results that have been delivered as time goes by. This can also be useful to communicate your plan and vision with any of your business' various stakeholders and employees.
2. Define what success looks like. It is important to be specific when defining success. This would be areas such as sales targets, income, costs, conversions, and page clicks on your website and social media platforms. You also need a plan to review progress, again being honest and specific, where you can track results and make changes where necessary. Either way, whether results are as expected, better than expected, or worse than expected, going through this process makes follow up and any action you need to take, a lot more timely and straightforward.
3. Put the plan into motion. As you deliver your business plan and review and update targets, you will be in a much better position to analyze the deliverables and the work that sits behind the numbers. This in turn means you will be in a better position to work out what is working and what is not working for you, your business, and your team.

This can be a daunting process at any stage of running your own business, but particularly if the business and entrepreneurial world is a completely new concept. So, it can help to break your plan into smaller more manageable stages. Entrepreneurs, at all stages of the business journey, can find this a helpful process by developing plans and then breaking them down into phases. The different time frames of the planning process place particular focus of the time-sensitive aspects of the business plans.

The way this would be broken down by most businesses is planning for the short, medium, and long term. Short-term plans would usually cover areas that could be achieved in a year, medium-term plan would cover areas that can be achieved in several years, and long-term plans would mean five years or more and are usually based on reaching medium-term targets. Doing your planning with this structure means you can focus on short-term plans with the long-term plans very much in mind.

Short-Term Planning

This looks at all features of the business in the present and the short term and sets objectives for improving them, for example, product quality issues or employee training. To address and resolve issues like these, short-term solutions can be put in place and in turn can also be a foundation for longer term solutions.

Short-term plans are geared toward things such as improving cash flow and launching a new product. Whatever the short-term goals are, make sure they serve the long-term plans. So, a new product launch should be consistent with the overall brand and in line with the product range you plan to build over time. Any strategy to improve cash flow should bring in additional revenue, but in such a way that does not detract from your long-term goals (e.g., not improving cash flow at the cost of cutting corners which can affect product quality).

Medium-Term Planning

This tends to be covering a time period of 18 months to 3 to 5 years. This applies more permanent solutions to short-term issues. Medium-term planning is there to introduce and implement procedures that ensure short-term problems don't reoccur in the future. This area is sometimes overlooked in the planning process, but is important, as it brings together the short-term plans with the depth of long-term plans.

Medium-term plans could include opening a new shop or office or entering a new market. Medium-term planning is a long enough time period to see if you are achieving the optimum results, but it is also short enough to amend or change direction if the initial strategy is not working.

Long-Term Planning

In the long term, which tends to be five years plus, businesses aim to solve problems permanently and achieve their overall objectives. Long-term planning looks at major capital expenses, implementing major policies and procedures, and develops strategies for adapting the business's position to achieve its long-term objectives. When short- and medium-term planning is successful, long-term planning looks to build on those successes and ensure that progress continues. Long-term plans would have the business mission statement as a guideline. Long-term goals need to be monitored and, in some cases, adjusted accordingly and have periodic benchmarks and milestones so progress can be continually evaluated.

Long-term goals could be to open a certain number of new premises over a set number of years. The difficulty can come with changing or volatile market conditions, making it harder to predict how the market will be over a longer time period. So long-term objectives may need to be less specific and encompassed by a larger vision. So rather than opening a set number of new premises, it could be encompassed by a vision to supply your product to specific regions. Long-term planning has to be taken seriously but may need reviewing and adjusting as the medium-term develops.

Having a clear business plan for the various time scales undoubtedly has many advantages. It gives an overview of the whole business, sets focus and priorities, allows for and encourages accountability, and sets key milestones and metrics. This is a template to refer back to and gives a structure to everything the business is looking to achieve. A worthwhile and valuable exercise that can set your business on the right track from the very beginning and gives the best possible chance to build a solid foundation for longevity and to allow for well-informed, high-quality plans for growth and expansion.

Planning without action is futile, action without planning is fatal.
—Cornelius Fichtner

CHAPTER 7

Networking and Social Media

You can't sell anything if you can't tell anything.
—Beth Comstock

Networking is the process of building and maintaining a mutually beneficial relationship with other business people as well as potential new customers and clients. While this allows you to tell other people about your business and hopefully win new clients, it is important to remember that it is equally about how you can help other your fellow business peers. The mutually beneficial aspect is all important; some opinions support the idea that giving is in fact a starting point in networking rather than what you can get. As with many things, it is about balance, but giving out the right impression is vital, and you want to give an impression of being equally interested in what you can do to help someone as well as what they can do to help you.

In any part of the entrepreneurial journey, it is absolutely essential to build, maintain, and grow a strong network. These days there are a number of ways to build a strong and effective network. A common saying in the business world is "your network is your net worth."

There are many different ways and means of networking, either face to face, at industry events, at networking events, or via social media. The good thing about this is in a lot of cases this can be done at a minimal or no financial cost. The key principle is getting yourself out there, using every possible means available and connecting and subsequently building effective and solid relationships with people. This may be out of your comfort zone, but it is a massively important part of business, particularly at the early stages and has to be done.

No matter what stage of the networking journey you are at, whether you have a strong list of contacts, starting from scratch or anything in between there are lots of new people to meet in the business world, many of whom may be in a similar position and many different ways to connect.

Face-to-Face Networking

There are numerous different ways of doing this. Nowadays, it is true that there are more and more business networking events that are available to entrepreneurs. Some are local and largely attended by local business owners and stakeholders, some are on a larger scale with larger attendances, and in some cases will have high-profile keynote speakers. Some entrepreneurs have started their own networking events businesses, where like-minded businesspeople can connect with each other.

This inevitably means increased choice, which has both advantages and disadvantages. More choice does mean you can pick and choose which events you go to; however, more choice can also mean varying levels of quality, and if you are going to take time out from the money-making tasks, you want to ensure you use your networking time wisely and productively. It is always worthwhile checking who will be at the event exhibiting or doing keynote speeches and that will give you an idea of the audience and who you are likely to meet. Ultimately, larger firms may well have a team of people who attend networking events; in some cases, this will be a large part of their full-time job. That is not a luxury that small business owners have, so research, time management, and prioritizing are particularly key in the early stages.

When attending these events, it is important to be fully prepared. In most cases, this is easy to do, and you will be able to research who will be at advertised events and what companies will be represented. The most common thing to swap with someone you meet is business cards; however, there is other promotional material you could also use depending on what type of business or industry that you are in. First impressions certainly count and if you say that you will be in touch, will connect on social media, or will follow up, it goes without saying that you should do what you have said you would. (It's amazing how many people do not, and you only have one chance to make a first impression.) This does not have to be with the view of making an immediate sale (a sale of any sort could take time but could certainly come later); again, it is with the intention of making connections and seeing how you can help each other. At times, it may be the case that you know someone who can help the person you are networking with. Either way it is all about making the initial, positive connection.

Social Media and Your Own Company Website

Many years ago, communication via businesses used to be done via telephone calls and letters in the mail. Nowadays, things are very different. The emergence and subsequent dominance of social media has added an enormous new dimension to how entrepreneurs can connect and network. So much so that nowadays you can build a business as a social media personality or influencer. As an entrepreneur, you can interact with people who have a large social media following, and in some cases, they can help. Furthermore, endorsements from celebrities or social media influencers can literally transform the fortunes of your business overnight. However, this can work both ways and either positively or negatively depending on what the celebrity, blogger, or influencer says about your product or service. Examples of well-known celebrity endorsements would be George Clooney and Nespresso, Taylor Swift and Diet Coke, Charlize Theron and Dior, Dwayne Johnson and Under Armour, David Beckham and Haig Club Whisky, and Michael Jordan and Nike. This type of endorsement can lead to an increase in direct sales, increased awareness of the product and brand, and increased confidence and loyalty. Ultimately, if your favorite sports player, actor, or celebrity wears a particular brand of clothing or shoe, it will resonate with their fan base and the wider population and will provide a point of differentiation from rival brands.

There are several different social media platforms that you can use to set up a personal profile and a business page to use to start networking, showcasing your business and what you do. This can also be used for advertising and converting networking into business.

Given the sheer volume of people who use these platforms, it is important for any type of business to have some sort of presence online. Given the potential wider audience, varied demographics per platform, potential new connections, networking opportunities, and ultimately business you can engage and attract, it is a "no brainer." On most social media platforms, you can create pages for no cost and have access to all of their millions of users.

There are some key principles to follow when using social media for your business:

- What is equally important to having an online presence is keeping your content up to date and continuing to be active across all of your platforms. Ultimately, there is no point in creating these accounts or a company website and not keeping them up to date and relevant or by posting regularly. An out-of-date website, or a social media platform that hasn't been used for a long period, is not a good look, a very poor first impression and certainly doesn't instill any confidence in your business.

- All of the platforms have a message facility. So, replying to messages in a timely and professional manner is another thing to consider. Again, it's not a good look to be contacted by a potential customer and for them not to receive a timely reply.

- Your content needs to be clear, engaging, concise, and consistent as well as regular. It is also important to make sure your content has substance and is consistent with your overall brand. It must appeal to the right audience, your target market, and link back to your key messages.

- There is a great deal of insight available about when is the optimum time to post on the various social media platforms, including when they have the highest number of users online to get highest number of views/interactions.

- If your posts and content sticks to these principles, it should attract a good mixture of "likes," comments, retweets, or shares, which will maximize its reach and influence. As a result, this should provide a good platform for networking and attracting new interest and new business.

With the various platforms available, managing social media can be a time-consuming thing to do; while your content needs to be high quality, time management and prioritization are important here. Where your social media activities go on, your list of priorities depends to some extent on the type of business you are running.

However, this is something that can be outsourced. With the growth of social media and its popularity, this has led to a lot of businesses that offer marketing services and essentially can do your social media activity for you. This can save time, but also you have to consider cost, what quality of service you will get, and how well someone else can represent your business.

There are many different ways this can be approached, but below is a more in-depth look at some of the different platforms that are available, ways that your online presence can be used and maximized.

LinkedIn: This is mainly a professional business platform where you can connect with current and former colleagues as well as connecting with new people. This is a key characteristic of LinkedIn that sets it apart from other platforms. It's a professional site and you have to keep this is mind when posting content. You can also contribute to industry-specific discussions and join groups where you can interact with peers from your own industry. You can setup your own business page and also write your own articles and post content either as marketing material or to promote interest in your business. All of these activities can lead to connecting to new people. LinkedIn currently has nearly 740 million members across 200 territories and countries worldwide.

Facebook: This platform has huge usage. On August 27, 2012, Facebook announced that one billion people had connected on the platform.

Brands and individuals are to post an unlimited amount of text as well as photos and videos.

Users can like and share posts as well as directly message individuals and businesses alike. A Facebook business page allows you to include opening hours, reviews, and contact information, which in some ways is a duplication of the content you would put on your company website.

Examples of brands:

Nike has over 35 million followers.
Manchester United has over 74 million followers.

Instagram: Another platform with a huge number of users—roughly one billion active users a month. Recently bought by Facebook, Instagram is the "less wordy" social media platform, where users upload photos or video content to share updates. People are attracted to visuals as well as words and brands have a big presence on Instagram and over 50 percent of Instagrammers follow brands. Instagram posts have to be visually stimulating and you have to be creative and captivating.

Examples of brands and individuals:

FC Barcelona has over 104 million followers.
Businessman, movie star, and Governor Arnold Schwarzenegger has over 22 million followers.
Disney has over 32 million followers.

Twitter: It is one of the oldest social media platforms but has over 314 million users with around 100 million users active daily. Setting up a company page is straightforward; however, the format of twitter is different to other platforms. There is currently a character limit on what you can post of 140 characters, but you can still have pictures, videos, and links in whatever you post. So, with this platform, there is an extra challenge of keeping your content short and succinct, while also getting across your key message.

Examples of brands and individuals:

Businessman and front man of the Apprentice in the U.K. Lord Alan Sugar has over five million followers.
U.S. businessman and a member of the panel on Shark Tank Mark Cuban has over eight million followers.
Starbucks has over 10 million followers.

YouTube: In some ways, YouTube could be seen as the heart of social media platforms because it is so widely distributed among the other platforms. For example, 400 tweets per minute contain a YouTube link. If video content is right for your business and brand and for getting your message out there, then having a YouTube channel is going to be worthwhile.

While this is a platform for some of the brands we have mentioned previously, it is also a platform that some have been able to use as a springboard to become "YouTubers"— people who make a living off posting videos which in itself is entrepreneurship. All YouTubers would have started from scratch, have had to build viewers and subscribers, and once you are at that stage, you can start making enough money to make a living.

For example:

PewDiePie is a video game commentator, showing reactions to him as he plays video games, has over 111 million subscribers and over 10 billion views.

Jenna Marbles, who posts videos about being a young millennial woman, has over 20 million subscribers and nearly two billion views.

TikTok: This is a relatively new platform, launched in 2017 for IOS and Android markets, that has gained an enormously increased profile in recent years. As of 2018, TikTok is available in 75 languages in over 150 markets. The app allows users to create and upload short videos that can be slowed down, sped up, or edited using a filter. Background music can also be added, and there is also a lip sync feature. In terms of business use, this app has allowed small businesses to advertise and reach consumers outside of the demographic that they would usually serve. In 2020, Shopify added TikTok to its social media platforms, which allowed online traders to sell directly to consumers on TikTok.

Having your own company website: Can any business get by without having its own website in today's world? In most cases, the answer would have to be a "no." This is an important consideration for any type and size of business, again in terms of research, costs, time management priorities, and whether this is something you may outsource. If you decide to have a website for your business, some of the things to consider would be:

1. *Naming your website:* This is your company's web address, and this is what people will type in to go to your business' website. There are a number of ways of registering a domain name with different

web hosting companies. Ideally you would want your website and business name to be the same, so it's a good idea to check and secure your domain name at the same time as naming your business. (You don't want to be in a position where you risk your domain name and business name being different.) You also have to decide on the suffix at the end of your domain name. The most common and usually most expensive is .com; however, there are others, such as .co.uk and .net. While you have to consider the cost, it may be an idea to register your domain name with multiple suffixes, and this will not only maximize chances of visitors finding the site but also protect the brand and guard against duplication, where two businesses have the same name, but one has .com and the other .co.uk.

2. *Building your website:* For the design and building of your website, this is something that can be done by yourself or by a professional. It largely depends on your knowledge and abilities in this area as well as time management and prioritization. Ultimately, you want the end result to be a professional job. A DIY job can be done at relatively low cost; however, the lower the cost, potentially there is less scope to make it look good and to customize. The more expensive packages allow you to have more pages, more scope for customizing, and things like company e-mail and online shops. Another area to consider is making sure your website can be viewed equally well on tablets and smartphones as well as on a computer. Both website building and design are specialist areas, so you may wish to get a dedicated web company to do this while you concentrate on other areas of the business. There are many different options here depending on budget and quality. Getting this choice right is important longer term as well; for example, if you do look at outsourcing, ideally you would stay with the same person as you go through expansion. A sound working relationship is always helpful, but having to swap web designers for whatever reason means starting the outsourcing process (and potentially your website) again from scratch.

3. *The content of your website:* Your website should be engaging, have good content, and be easy to navigate. Ultimately, if it attracts new visitors, you want people to want to stay on there and have a look around. If the first impression is not right, then the chances are they

won't return for a second look. It is important that the content itself is clear, concise, and relevant and represents the business brand. A mixture of posts, updates, blogs, and vlogs as well as keeping the site up to date is important to maintain engagement. A weekly or monthly newsletter is also an option. Another key consideration is double checking for any spelling mistakes and making sure that your contact details are correct. There is only one chance to make a first impression.

4. *Attracting visitors:* One of the key things to do here is to make sure your website appears on all of your different marketing materials; for example, social media pages, business cards, letterheads, the signature on your e-mail, and any promotional goods you may use such as mugs, mouse mats, or pens. As well as ensuring you have a good-quality content, it is important to make sure you keep updating your website, possibly including blogs, vlogs, and latest news from you and possibly your industry. This can then be used to circulate around your posts on social media platforms, making sure that what you post links back to your website. Search engine optimization is also important here. This concept, also known as "SEO," covers techniques that can be used to improve a website's performance in search engine rankings. This includes optimizing your site to perform well for specific keywords around your business. Other SEO techniques involve writing relevant content to go on your website. There are also "pay per click" services that allow you to buy your way to the top of search engines results for relevant search phrases for your business. There are a few different providers of this service and there are costs attached.

Building on Your Existing Network

You never know how someone you know, may know someone who can offer advice or help you out. When you decide to embark on your entrepreneurial adventure, tell people you know, your friends and family, your business network. They may be able to help, or they may well know someone or knows someone who knows someone who may be able to help in some way.

The benefits of business networking:

- *New contacts and referrals:* This is arguably the primary benefit of networking. New contacts can also lead to opportunities for joint ventures, partnerships, or new areas for expansion for the business.
- *Visibility:* You need to meet and build relationships with potential clients and generate referrals so you can continue to generate new business. Attending the right type of networking events will connect you to the right people, and regular attendance will keep you at the forefront of the right people's minds.
- *Problem solving:* As well as gaining new business, networking can help you find solutions for your own business challenges or needs. For example, if your business needs an accountant, funding options, HR advice, administration assistance, or legal advice, this can be easily found by networking. Alternatively, if you are looking for investment, then this can also be found via networking. These relationships can be established and can be beneficial, potentially for the long term.
- *Sharing knowledge and experiences:* Another key benefit is sharing knowledge and experience of other businesspeople and sharing your experiences with them. Taking advantage of the experience of others or sharing your experience can be invaluable and can save a lot of time and money. For example, if you are thinking of starting to import or export internationally, or taking on new staff, talking through the mechanics of this with someone who has experience in this area can be a massive help.
- *Staying up to date:* The only real certainty in the modern business world is uncertainty. It is important for any entrepreneur to keep up to date with changes in market conditions and market trends. Knowing your market is also key to having a well-thought-out business and marketing plan. If you have employees or your own premises, there may be HR and health and safety legislation you need to stay familiar with.

Attending networking events with your peers in your industry will on a regular basis will help you keep on top of market changes.

- *Increased morale and confidence:* Regularly associating with like-minded businesspeople can be a moral boost at all times, but particularly in the early stages. It can also help boost your confidence, particularly if you are not a naturally outgoing person, to go out of your comfort zone and ultimately build new and effective relationships with your business peers.

Networking is marketing. Marketing yourself, your uniqueness, what you stand for.

—Christine Lynch

CHAPTER 8

Marketing

Good marketing makes the company look smart. Great marketing makes the customer feel smart.

—Joe Chernov

Marketing is the process of getting current or potential clients or customers interested in the product or services that your business offers. The process involves research and promotion and selling, but ultimately, it is with the intention of getting your product or service and your customers together.

Marketing is a vital part of any business and is a key ingredient that will help maximize the chance of success. In today's competitive business environment, it is a requirement to set yourself apart from the crowd as much as possible and to stand out. Most businesses will have a marketing strategy of some kind in place. This goes hand in hand with a universal objective of businesses which is to sell their products or services.

It is good practice for any business in any sector should have a clear marketing plan in place with the intention of setting themselves apart from the competition. The plan would look to outline how you will effectively reach potential clients or customers and keep in touch with your current customer and client base.

The good news is that there are many different ways of marketing your business, with varying degrees of cost, appropriateness, and effectiveness. This is partly dependent on what sort of business you run as well as more practical elements such as money and resources.

So, all businesses sell something—a product or a service that solves a problem. It is of critical importance that any entrepreneur can identify their business market and as a result identify their target audience.

Marketing is much more than just advertising. Just "placing a few adverts" is not sufficient and, in all likelihood, will not generate the kind of business a small business, or indeed any-sized business, needs to be successful. While advertising is a big part of marketing, a full marketing strategy is a process that needs planning and regular review and modifying. That does not mean it needs to be complicated, it's just something that needs proper planning, thorough research, regular review and updating, and perseverance.

There are some basic strategies that you could use to "get the ball rolling" and use as a foundation to increase awareness of your business. These types of strategies are helpful at any time, but are particularly useful in the early stages.

- *Offering some free workshops or classes:* Something like this particularly in the early stages can be a good place to start. A class, presentation, or workshop, with no charge, that is related to what product or service you are trying to sell can be beneficial initially to get yourself out there and increase awareness.
- *Join business networking groups or organizations:* This is a great option to make contact with like-minded professionals and potential clients or customers. The marketing benefits of this can be potentially huge in terms of getting new business contacts and connecting with new customers. (Networking is covered in more detail in Chapter 7.)
- *Create or take part in charity events:* This is an opportunity for positive coverage that can increase awareness of what you do, your personal brand, and in turn translate to customers. This doesn't have to be creating your own event necessarily; you can get involved by sponsoring an event or supporting it in another way. This can be a "double win" where you can support a great cause and also achieve some good publicity and increase awareness.
- *Start a blog:* Having your own blog can be a great way to build an audience and awareness of what products or services you offer. Writing regularly and with clear and high quality about your industry and what your business is doing can lead to you connecting with fellow bloggers, businesspeople, and potential customers.

- *Get on social media:* This is a massive area, with a variety of different platforms and literally millions of people that you can reach and share your business with. Picking your platforms and having a clear succinct message is important, but this is certainly an opportunity to reach a massive amount of people with a relatively low cost and time investment. (Social media is covered in more detail in Chapter 7.)
- *Get referrals:* This is particularly useful if you are running a business that provides a service. Never be afraid to ask for feedback or a referral. Word of mouth is powerful, and this is a straightforward way to spread the word.

Types of Business Market

Business-to-consumer (B2C) market: In this type of market, a business focuses on selling its goods or services to individual customers, clients, and consumers. When businesses buy something, one of the main considerations will be bottom-line impact and return on investment (ROI). Selling a product or service to a business can be complicated and time consuming in some cases. For example, if you are trying to sell to a larger business, you will need to find out who the relevant decision maker is, make contact with them, and arrange a meeting to get your foot in the door (potentially, this process can take a while!).

Business-to-business (B2B) market: This type of market focuses on goods or services that are sold to other businesses rather than individual consumers. There are some cases where B2B markets can overlap with B2C markets. For example, an office furniture company can sell goods to other businesses and to individual consumers. As opposed to B2B marketing, which focuses largely on bottom-line impact, B2C marketing doesn't necessarily consider the financial risks as much as a business would be inclined to.

The services market: In this market, a business sells services rather than products. This could be an electrician, plumber, or builder selling exclusively to consumers. It could also be a B2B firm selling accountancy, training, or consultancy services. There are some examples of businesses that may sell a product in conjunction with the service. An example of this could be a hairdresser who sells hair gel and coloring products as well as haircuts.

The industrial market: This type of market sells industrial or production products, goods, and services to various different industries. This type of product is not usually marketed to consumers. They are usually goods such as wood, steel, and other raw materials or larger scale goods. This type of market also has a smaller target audience as the type of goods and services it supplies are not mass market focused.

The professional services market: This type of market includes professional services that require some sort of license or certification. This type of business could be a law firm, a dentist, or medical firm. As with the B2B market, there can sometimes be an overlap where a business sells to both businesses and consumers. For example, a law firm can provide representation to another business as well as an individual.

Creating a Marketing Plan

As with many aspects of running a business, you must properly plan how you will approach your marketing before you put it into practice to ensure it is effective—a sound plan enables clear decision making and helps to establish tasks, to create reasonable deadlines, and to maintain focus. Research is a key part of this process, and you should ask yourself:

- How will the marketing plan help my business goals? Before you start putting a plan together, you need to be specific and to be sure about what you want to achieve from your marketing. Your marketing strategy is directly connected to your overall business objectives. Having a time frame is also important for your marketing plan to keep it measured and realistic and to review performance and effectiveness. Benchmarking is important here to measure ROI in your marketing strategy.

- Who is my target market? This is the group of people who make up the specific audience to whom you want to sell your product or service to. Market research of this area is vital. The more specific you are with establishing who your target market is or is likely to be, the more targeted your marketing plan will be. It is important to research: Who is your target audience? Where can you find them? What is important to them and what are they worried about? What do they need and when do they need it? Having an idea of what sort of business you would wish to work with helps identify specifics about your customer base and also personalize your marketing message.

- Who is my competition? This is another area of market research and an important aspect here is knowing who your key competitors are. In terms of marketing, researching who your competitors sell to, what they are doing well, and what you could do in a better or more effective way are vital areas to look at. This is another area where a SWOT analysis (covered in more detail in Chapter 2) could be carried out, both on your competitors and your own business' marketing strategy.

- How will you reach your target market? There are many ways in which this can be done. For example, advertising via leaflets, social media, sales materials, marketing materials, cold calling, direct mail, sales promotions, industry-specific events, or other various publicity or networking events. This ties into understanding who your target market and customers are and that in turn will help decide which is the best way to reach them. There is a lot of choice in terms of how to do this, choosing a few and doing them effectively is better than doing them all ineffectively.

- What is the cost and time implications? Cost is another key area, particularly in the early stages of your business. You always need to consider and review budgeting for all areas of your business including your marketing activities. Knowing what your budget is will help to inform what marketing activities you can afford to put in place. Having an annual budget is good practice, and it is also worth breaking it down into monthly budgets. This allows you to track results more closely, and as a result, you can modify your approach if necessary to make sure you are maximizing ROI.

- Create an action list: Having a plan of what you need to do and when is a key part of this process will help you stay on track. Similarly, with any plan, it is important to have a specific end goal and work out the steps to get there. An example of this would be setting a marketing goal of delivering 3,000 leaflets by the end of the month. The steps to achieve this could include determining your budget, sourcing suppliers, and planning when you can deliver the leaflets to hit your deadline.

- What are your metrics? All of the work you put into your plan will be less useful if you do not have metrics to measure effectiveness. The way you track this depends on what type of marketing you are using. For example, if you are using social media, you will be able to track using each sites analytics; however, if you are doing offline marketing, more traditional tracking methods will be needed. By measuring your metrics, you will be able to have a much greater understanding of where you have the most success and opportunities with your marketing, and as a result of this insight, you will be able to tailor your activities accordingly.

There are a number of marketing activities that are available, with different financial and time costs. A mixture of these may be appropriate depending on what conclusions you have drawn from your research and marketing plan:

- *Paid advertising:* This is any type of advertising that you have to pay the owner of the advertising space for use of that space. It can include advertising in local or regional newspapers or magazines, TV advertising, and "pay per click" advertising on the Internet. If used effectively, this can be an effective way of getting your business out there to a large audience relatively quickly.

- *Internet marketing:* This is marketing your business over various platforms using various approaches on the Internet (social media is covered in more detail in Chapter 7) and using tools that help drive leads, traffic, and sales. Internet marketing is a broad term that encompasses a range of strategies including content, search, e-mail, and paid media. This is one of the least expensive ways to reach your target market, irrespective of your business size, and can be very effective if used effectively, and when your content is really succinct and effective, it makes a massive difference—good-quality and well-planned blogs, infographics, podcasts, case studies, and videos can all help contribute to an effective Internet marketing strategy.

- *Word of mouth:* Undoubtedly, it is a very powerful marketing tool. It is triggered completely by a positive (or negative) customer experience and is ultimately down to the impression you leave people with. When you give a high-quality service and product to a client or consumer, they are more likely to recommend you. Everything from the start of the customer journey has to be right. This is an organic way of getting positive reviews out there, by making a bond with people, so they will refer friends and family (and is completely free of charge).

- *Relationship marketing:* This is where you look to build customers, enhance current relationships, and look to improve customer loyalty. This focuses on creating, building, and establishing a long-term relationship with the customer and recognizing their long-term value. So, this strategy goes beyond sales promotion and focuses on areas such as customer satisfaction and retention.

- *Transactional marketing:* This is where a business would focus on selling and potentially use events, sales, or coupons to encourage larger volume sales and encourage the target audience to buy the promoted products. An example of this type of promotion would be to offer 50 percent for your 100th customer. This type of marketing tends to focus on "one-off" transactions and individual sales as opposed to creating an ongoing, long-term relationship with the customer.

- *Cause marketing:* This is where a business service or product is linked to a good cause or an important social issue. So, in essence, this is a combination of looking to better society and increase profitability. One example of cause marketing could be being asked to make a one-off charitable donation at a checkout counter.
- *Undercover marketing:* This is where consumers see a product while remaining unaware of the marketing strategy. So, here you would be introducing a product or service to customers in a way that does not seem like actual marketing or advertising.

It is fair to say that marketing is something that has to be done to some degree, irrespective of the size of your business or the industry in which it operates. It is simply not an option to not make use of marketing. The balance comes when deciding what type of marketing to use and how much time and money you want or need to spend. This is where the size and industry of your business becomes important in deciding what marketing strategy fits best in your circumstances.

The best marketers are always creating relationships. Relationships with customers, brands and other marketers.

—Kurt Ulhir

CHAPTER 9

Understanding Key Financial Statements

If you don't have regular and accurate financial statements, you're driving your business 100 mph down a one way street the wrong way, at night, in the fog, without lights.

—Jim Blasingame

Understanding the key financial numbers associated with your business is critical and can make or break your venture. Having a strong grasp of what amount of money goes out and what comes in and the overall financial health of your business can be as daunting as it is necessary.

Ultimately, a business is started to make a profit and to make a living for the entrepreneur who started it. Any business needs to make more than it spends to sustain itself and to be successful. That means understanding and controlling the levels of spending and setting a fair and reasoned price point, making sure that you sell enough of a product or service at the right price to ensure enough income to cover your spending and support the business operations.

All of the various financial statements bring a business to life and give its performance some real context. This in turn will help make informed decisions about the running of a business and about what happens next. In terms of expanding a business, having solid and sustainable finances will provide an excellent foundation to build on.

The Key Stakeholders

The following stakeholders will (and should) take a keen and vested interest in your business' financial statements:

- *The business owner(s):* As mentioned earlier, the business owner(s) need to have a full and comprehensive understanding of the relevant financial statements. This ensures a full understanding of business performance and makes it easier to make informed business decisions.
- *Any investors:* If external funding from an investor was sought in the early stages or to fund expansion, then the investor will take a keen and regular interest in business performance. This is to make sure that their investment is being used wisely and to judge their potential rate of return.
- *Lenders:* Similarly in the early stages or to fund expansion, a loan could have been used. As with investors, any lender will want to make sure that their money is safe and being used sensibly and that the business has the capability to repay it.
- *Competitors:* In any competitive marketplace, there will be mutual interest in each business's financial health. Depending on circumstances, this could lead to opportunities for mergers or takeovers.
- *Employees:* Whether a business employs 1 person or 1,000 people or more, they have a responsibility to their employees. So, employees will take an interest in the financial health of their employers. If a business has strong and sustainable finances, that can increase employee confidence and may encourage them to stay long term. Similarly, if things start to look financially unsettled, there is a risk that employees may lose confidence and look for employment elsewhere.
- *Customers:* Will want clarity on the viability of the business before dealing with you and expect products or services to at least meet or exceed expectations.
- *Suppliers:* In many types of businesses, there is some degree of reliance on external suppliers. Each of those suppliers will need to be paid, so they will take an interest in the financial health of the businesses that they work with. Ultimately, if any of them hit financial turbulence, there is a risk that someone will not be paid on time.
- *The government and tax authorities:* Any business that generates funds will have to complete accounts and declare their

income to government. This is to ensure that the correct level of tax can be paid.

Whether you are a "natural" or not, you need to have an understanding of the various financial figures and what they mean for you, your business, and you stakeholders. To begin with, let's define two key terms.

Financial Accounting

This is where your financial statements are prepared for you and all your key stakeholders.

Other key stakeholders may include your accountant, your employees, your bank, any partner businesses and suppliers, the HMRC, and current and potential customers or clients.

The rules and regulations around this vary in different countries. Broadly speaking, if your business is a limited company, it is a legal obligation to submit regular updates of your financial statements, and if you are self-employed, you are likely to have to do some sort of tax self-assessment. The rules are important and have to be adhered to, if not there are likely to be penalties.

The areas of detail that are included in financial accounting are information on your business's performance (i.e., profit or loss), it's financial position (e.g., assets, liability, and equity), and any key changes to the financial position.

Management Information

This includes your financial metrics that will help you manage your business more efficiently and effectively.

This information will therefore facilitate your effective decision making and should underpin planning and ongoing business strategy.

Examples include the following:

- A purchase ledger to make payments to creditors and suppliers
- A sales ledger to invoice for the sales made to your customers or clients

Budgeting and Planning for Your Business

Budgeting is needed because all businesses have finite resources. Budgeting is therefore about making clear, measured, and informed choices for your business. Where you decide what you want to do with the resources that are available to you.

There are many types of budgets, each of which will contribute to your business strategies. Examples of budgets you may use include sales, cash flow, production, marketing, and project budgets.

Budgeting is usually done on a yearly cycle and will indicate:

- You have a clear understanding of the resources required for your key business activities.
- You can proceed with making key decisions knowing that the resources are available to carry out these activities.

The need to forecast is closely aligned with budgeting processes. Forecasting is where you predict/project how much resource will be required and when it will be required. Key resources will include finance, equipment, and people.

Therefore, budget planning should be an integral aspect of your business operations, where you look to:

- Start off by considering your intended activities for the designated planning period.
- Have a clear understanding of what you are looking to achieve and how you will achieve it.
- Work out resource availability, requirements, and capacity.
- Understand the total cost associated with the resources required.

Given the finiteness of your business's capacity, robust budgetary control mechanisms must be in place. Having a budget means clear visibility of what resource has been allowed and used for a specific activity of your business. It also means you can readily and easily see what happens (e.g., actual resource requirements against budget). Clearly, any deviations need to be identified, investigated, and understood; then any appropriate adjustments can be made to the budget.

The Benefits of Budgeting

Control: A budget means you can have more control over how, where, and when you allocate the resources you have available. You can, for example, spread your expected resource requirements for the months or year ahead. It is important that your budget is regularly reviewed and updated to accommodate any unforeseen changes in internal and external circumstances.

Guidance: Your budget enables you to continually develop and inform your decision-making process. You can readily see how you have made decisions about resource allocation for the various activities of your business. As a result, you are then better equipped to understand the business' resource priorities.

Capacity planning: Your business will have inevitable resource constraints, so your entrepreneurial skills must include the optimum allocation and use of the available capacity.

Understanding: Reality determines that nothing stays constant, so any of your budgetary predictions will soon be challenged in some way. It is therefore vital that your business has a robust and reliable process to track actual budget/resource activity against what was planned. There can be many reasons for a variance, including:

- Incorrect budget or resource allocation at the outset
- Unrealistic expectations as to what could be delivered from the initial set budget
- Unexpected or unplanned changes outside of your control
- Poor cost and resource management which leads to increased and unnecessary additional expense

Creating a Budget

When you create your budget, this will be an iterative process where you most likely begin with your principal budget factor. This term is also known as the limiting budget factor or key budget factor; by clear implication, however termed, this factor gives clear parameters for all activities of your business, for example, sales, material/stock, and people.

Clarification of Costs

- *Fixed costs:* These are the costs of your business that remain constant over a certain period, usually defined as 12 months or more. These costs remain constant irrespective of changes in your business's activities or levels of production.

Therefore, whether your business has a zero output or record levels of output, the level of fixed costs will remain broadly constant. Over the longer term, fixed costs can change. Possibilities include increased overheads or an investment in your production capacity. Examples of fixed costs include mortgage payments, insurance, or rent.

- *Variable costs:* The costs that vary as your business activity levels change. So, these costs vary directly with the level of activity and production and are output-related inputs. Examples include wages, fuel, utilities, and other revenue-related costs like commission.
- *Semivariable costs:* Sometimes known as semifixed costs and are those costs that aren't directly correlated to any level of business activity, yet can still change over time. Examples include maintenance costs and depreciation of machinery.
- *Direct costs:* Any costs that are readily identifiable and attributable to a specific product or service are direct costs, for example, material and labor costs. Direct costs are therefore any costs that clearly contribute to business activities (i.e., production of products or services). A direct cost can also be classified as a variable cost if it regularly fluctuates.
- *Indirect costs:* Any costs that cannot be directly allocated to business activities and will vary with output (i.e., production). These costs are more difficult to assign to a specific product or service. Examples may include quality control, maintenance, depreciation, and administration.

Cash Flow Accounts

This account shows exactly what the name implies—How much cash comes into and goes out of your business. It therefore follows that to be sustainable, any business needs to have an overall positive cash flow. Meaning that over time, there will be more cash coming into your business than going out.

This account, when used in conjunction with other financial statements, can help you to understand and manage your business's performance.

We also need to be clear that a positive cash flow is a significantly different financial indicator to profitability. Your profitability levels are calculated via your profit and loss account (this is outlined later in the chapter). That is, from day 1 it is essential to grasp that those levels of profit do not necessarily equate to or guarantee survival. Your business must have adequate cash to maintain liquidity.

However, your cash flow account is important because you can readily see how much cash you have available to meet various ongoing financial obligations. Potentially your business may be able to survive for the short term without sales or profit. However, there will be an ongoing requirement for cash.

An unfortunate reality is that many start-ups will fail because of poor cash flow scrutiny and monitoring. This can also be a risk when going through expansion.

Calculating Your Cash Flow

Your cash flow is basically a calculation:

- The money which flows into your business on a given day, less the money which flows out.
- The ongoing balance is what was left from the day before (either a credit or debit cash flow balance).
- Your aim is to ensure you have enough cash (ideally plus a margin) to honor your day-to-day financial commitments.
- Your cash flow document is ideally sectioned into meaningful blocks and subtotals. This clarity of structure is vital, so you can readily obtain clear information on the cash movements in your business.

Later, we will consider a range of methods to be adopted which will speed up your cash inflows and minimize your cash outflows.

Components of Your Cash Flow

Overall, in this context, cash embraces a range of components all of which are normal trading activities:

- Cash (notes and coins)
- Credit card payments
- Electronic money transfers, for example, via PayPal
- Mobile technology payments
- Checks (though these aren't common these days)

Income

The primary source of cash coming into your business is most likely to be from sales of products or services. Therefore, if you purchase on credit, you should aim to sell your product or service before payment is due. Clearly if you offer credit terms on your sales, make sure your business can cover this delay until payment is received. Ideally, you will be paid in cash and buy on credit (though this is not always reality).

Another potential source of income for your business could be new finance: for example, an investment from your business partner or a bank loan. Either of these circumstances will provide a one-off boost to your cash flow.

Outgoings

The main outflow of cash will be the costs that are necessary to run and sustain your business: for example, office overheads and colleague salaries.

There may be occasional larger outgoings, when, for example, you need to purchase more stock, raw materials, or new machinery.

Perhaps, the purpose of your business will mean that for the short term, any work-in progress will need to be funded. For example, a designer may spend several months on a project before it's ready to sell. So, in the meantime, the materials, labor, and other fundamental activities will need to be funded prior to payment.

Cash Flow Forecasting

A cash flow is primarily historic, representing aspects of your business's performance in the recent past. It is always useful and probably essential to develop, say, monthly cash flow forecasts.

Benefits of cash flow forecasting include the following:

- Indicating to your key stakeholders that you are managing your business responsibly.
- Giving you a clearer understanding of your business's financial performance—Knowing and understanding your numbers is so important!
- You can see when you may need additional funding, most likely for the short term. For example, when cash out exceeds cash in, an overdraft facility may be a viable short-term option to maintain liquidity. Other possible scenarios include making greater profits, reducing stock levels, improving your debtor management, or increasing your creditors.
- Inconsistencies in your business's performance can be more easily identified.
- Your actual cash flow can be compared to your forecasts so that deviances can be identified, and you can then take the appropriate course of action to remedy the situation. Once you have an established and reliable cash flow process, it must be regularly reviewed and updated. The information contained in your cash flow needs to be accurate and inclusive.

Understanding and managing your cash flow can ultimately be your critical success (or failure) factor. This aspect needs to be constantly reviewed so that you realize very early on if your business's funding strategies need to be changed.

Break-Even Analysis

A break-even analysis expressly reveals the levels of product or service that you need to sell to cover your costs.

So, this is where your revenue generated from sales covers your fixed and variable costs, where you make neither profit or loss.

Examples of fixed costs, which are not related directly to the volume of production, could be administration costs, research and development, and rental costs and rates.

Examples of variable costs, which change when production output changes, could be costs of raw materials, labor, fuel, and revenue-related costs such as commission.

Profit and Loss Accounts

As an entrepreneur or business leader, it is essential that you understand your continuing profit or loss situation. This is usually done on a monthly, quarterly, or annual basis.

Effectively your profit and loss account looks at your business's income and expenditure. Your net financial position will be in either profit or loss for the given period.

Therefore, this financial statement shows where your business's incomes and gains are credited and expenses and losses debited. It is a list of all the ins and outs from your business. So, sales less costs.

Your profit and loss account can also be known as your P&L, income and expense statement, or income statement.

This account will include your incomes and credits, including sales turnover and debits, including allowances, cost of sales, and other overheads.

As a result, you can see how your business is performing in terms of sales and expenses.

Your profit and loss account has particular significance as it used to calculate your income and corporation taxes. These calculations need to be accurate because if they are submitted incorrectly there can be severe consequences (which can include added interest and financial penalties).

The completion of your profit and loss account means your key stakeholders have an awareness of your business's profitability over that specific accounting period.

For example, potential investors will want to see how well your business is performing and will heavily scrutinize all your financial statements prior to a lending decision.

Key Terms

Net income: Means your income/revenue after the cost of goods/services sold, other expenses and taxes have been deducted.

Gross profit: Refers to your income/revenue less the direct cost of goods/services sold. This is a crucial metric which indicates the financial well-being of your business.

Operating profit: This is your profit after all operational expenses (e.g., rent) are taken off gross profit. Nota Bene (NB): This calculation excludes tax liabilities and interest.

Net profit: This is your final figure, what is left after everything else has been deducted. That is, after all remaining expenses have been deducted from gross profit (e.g., tax liabilities)

Understanding the Cost of Sales

- The first entry is your sales figure, sometimes called turnover or income. This figure is the total amount of all the sales invoices over the last accounting period.
- Then, the costs of sales need to be deducted, also referred to as the cost of goods sold. These costs could typically embrace materials, machinery costs, and the people resource, that is, factory/production costs.

You can calculate a useful percentage of sales figure by dividing cost of sales by sales. This means comparisons can be made to businesses like your own, so you can have an idea of what could realistically be expected.

- Other costs are then deducted so that you can calculate your operating profit. These costs cover any expenses not considered as a cost of sale. These costs are more general and may include personnel costs, office costs, and marketing and advertising costs,

- So far then you would have been able to calculate your business's operating profit.
- Over time you may need to consider loans and other borrowing to support your ambition for business growth. This will mean interest will become payable. Interest payments will need to be honored, so affordability needs to be considered. To take a simple example, if your operating profit was £1,000 and interest £200, the interest could be paid five times over. You could say your "interest cover" was 5. In any circumstances where your business borrows, there must be positive interest cover as you arrive at your profit before tax (PBT) metric.
- Finally, you need to deduct your estimated or actual tax liabilities. Income must be available to meet your business's tax obligations as the tax authorities are primary creditors. Once tax is deducted, you have your profit after tax (PAT) metric.
- What you are left with is your retained profit, or perhaps in some future years your retained loss. Your retained profit is then available to support your plans for growth.

The Balance Sheet

Your balance sheet is a snapshot of all your business's assets and liabilities at that moment in time. It is a snapshot of your entire business at the close of business on a specific day. This means the figures are correct at only that precise moment time.

In most cases, your balance sheet will be produced concurrently with your profit and loss account.

The assets are everything that has a financial value that is owned by your business or is owed to it. Assets may include machinery, premises, stock/inventory, equipment, cash, and debtors.

The liabilities are everything that is owed by your business to one of your key stakeholders. Liabilities may include creditors, tax, overdrafts, and loans.

The difference between your business's assets and liabilities is its value to you, the owner. So, if you were to sell off all the assets and pay of all the liabilities, what is left is known as the "net worth" of your business.

All the assets and liabilities are shown at their historic cost, that is, their original cost to your business. Remember that a balance sheet includes only costs and as a result cannot represent the value of your business.

Current Assets

Current assets are cash or near to cash that is owed to your business, usually within a period of 12 months.

The main categories of current assets include the following:

- *Cash:* Which means cash in hand (on your business premises) or held with your financial services provider. This normally includes cash deposits with a notice period of less than 12 months. Cash is the most liquid of your current assets.
- *Debtors:* These are your customers or clients who have been invoiced and are yet to make payment. In most cases (ideally all), your business will agree terms of payment, often being integrated into the contract. Your business could expect to agree terms of debtor payment between 30 and 90 days. You will probably find your debtors are your business's largest current asset, so they need to be closely monitored and controlled. The emphasis is for your customers/debtors to pay you on time to facilitate liquidity.
- *Stock/inventory:* This is your business's work-in progress. This could be goods held, perhaps as raw materials, incomplete goods, or finished goods ready for sale. Finished goods are safer assets as they have a higher value and are more liquid. However, overall, stock is the least liquid current asset as it is further away from cash.

- *Prepayments:* These are any payments that are made in advance of receipt of goods or services, so technically belong in the next accounting period. An example could be if your business makes an advanced payment of 24 months' rent. This is a prepayment on your balance sheet because it is an amount owed to your business.
- *Refunds not yet received:* At one time your business may be due a refund, for example, value-added tax (VAT), tax, or other monies.

Current Liabilities

Current liabilities are those payments due to be made by your business in the next 12 months.

The main categories of current liabilities include the following:

- *Creditors:* This means what is owed to your suppliers, usually under the terms of trade or formal contractual arrangements.
- *Accruals:* These are the value of goods and services received by your business though yet to be paid for (i.e., the invoice from your supplier is yet to be received).
- *Tax:* The taxation system and legislation varies from country to country. Your business may charge VAT to your clients and pay corporation tax to the authorities.
- *Short-term debt:* For example, a bank overdraft facility. This is a current liability and legally it is repayable on demand. Also, any repayment toward a long-term debt that is due in the next 12 months is also a current liability.

Fixed or Noncurrent Assets

Your business's fixed or noncurrent assets:

- Belong to your business
- Have an expected usage for at least 12 months

The features of these fixed or noncurrent assets include the following:

- They are for regular use: for example, premises, machinery, vehicles, leases.
- Tangibility, which means they can be seen, touched, and felt. Premises and vehicles are again included here.
- Intangibility, meaning they exist on paper or electronically. This aspect includes goodwill, trademarks, copyrights, patents, and licenses.
- Appreciation, where these assets hold, possibly increase in value. Freehold property may fall into this category. NB: Appreciation value cannot be considered until the time of sale and for the interim period will be balanced out via a notional liability (i.e., a revaluation reserve).
- Depreciation, where the value of assets decreases over time. So, depreciation writes off the cost of an asset over time, over its effective useful life. Possibilities here include computer equipment, vehicles, and machinery. NB: Your business accounts will need to show the original costs of your fixed assets, along with their cumulative depreciation.

So, your business's fixed assets will be shown at cost less depreciation. This is often called the net book value.

For example, if you acquired a new computer at £5,000 with a useful life of three years. The annual depreciation will be £1,000. The computers valuation will therefore be written down to £4,000 after one year, £3,000 after two years, and £2,000 after three years.

Depreciation spreads the cost of a fixed asset over its lifetime. There is no residual value and neither is it an approach to provide funding for a replacement.

Goodwill

This means the value attached to your business's reputation, good name, and customers or clients. Goodwill can be calculated by taking the value of your business's assets from the potential sale price. It is effectively a premium added to the value of your business if it were to be sold.

Noncurrent Liabilities

This category will include amounts payable by your business more than 12 months from the balance sheet date:

- *Loans:* Any loan repayment due in the next 12 months is included as a current liability. The residual amount (i.e., what is due after a 12-month period) will be categorized as a non-current liability.
- *NB:* Any overdraft can be called up (i.e., repayment demanded anytime) and therefore is included as a current liability.
- *Debenture:* It is a loan that is formally documented and refers to a loan specifically taken out by your business. A debenture or loan can be unsecured or can be secured against a specific asset of your business.
- *Director's loan:* This could be where you loan money to your business in its early days to facilitate liquidity. Once your business is established and is sustainably solvent, the director's loan can be repaid.
- The purpose of splitting your business's liabilities into current and long-term categories is so you can see how readily immediate and short-term debts can be accommodated.

Interpreting Your Business's Financial Data

In this chapter, we have explored how to build your key financial statements. In a lot of ways, this is only the beginning because of greater significance is the need to understand what they all mean—illustrating and evaluating their importance for your business. It is essential to bring these figures to life.

There are a series of ratios which can be used that will facilitate your business planning and control.

These ratios can be allocated to three main areas:

- Profitability
- Liquidity
- Efficiency

Profitability Ratios

These are known as the control ratios for your business and quantify the long-term investment in your business. In other words, considering:

- The return on capital employed (ROCE)
- How far your sales contribute to the fixed costs of your business, subsequently revealing what remains as profit

Return on Capital Employed (ROCE)

- Firstly, calculate your net capital employed (total assets—current liabilities)
- You can then calculate your gross profit as a percentage of your net capital employed as follows:

$$\frac{\text{Gross profit} \times 100}{\text{Net capital employed}}$$

This ratio, especially when available over several years (as your business gets established), is a key indication of your level of control over your business's operations.

You are also able to calculate your net profit as a percentage of your net capital employed (also known as the primary ratio) as follows:

$$\frac{\text{Net profit} \times 100}{\text{Net capital employed}}$$

This ratio is of particular interest as it indicates the overall return on the long-term investment in your business. Should you wish, while the correlation will never be linear, you can compare your primary ratio percent with the returns you would achieve from investing your money in a different way (e.g., with a financial services organization such as a bank or investment firm).

- When you consider your gross profit as a percentage of sales, you have a measure of the difference between the buying price and selling price of your goods or services.

This ratio is calculated as below:

$$\frac{\text{Gross profit} \times 100}{\text{Sales}}$$

As with all of your financial metrics, they have greater context when considered as a trend, over a number of years. This ratio confirms your business's markup—the amount added to the cost price to obtain the selling price of your product or service. This markup must be appropriate to cover all your running costs and profit.

- If you then consider net profit as a percentage of sales, you quantify what is left for profit after all other expenses have been covered.

We can calculate as follows:

$$\frac{\text{Net profit} \times 100}{\text{Sales}}$$

It is therefore critical that this ratio is monitored carefully, to see whether it is improving or reducing over time.

Liquidity Ratios

In this range of ratios, you gain an understanding of your business's ability to meet its short- and long-term obligations—in a nutshell, its ability to pay its way.

As with all your other ratios and financial metrics, in isolation, they add minimal value. Nevertheless, by considering trends and realistic comparisons, you can then gain a more realistic understanding of your business's liquidity.

The current ratio is where you compare your current assets (cash or near to cash coming into your business) against your current liabilities (cash or near to cash going out of your business), expressed as a ratio to 1.

This ratio is of vital importance as it demonstrates your business's ability to meet its day-to-day (i.e., very short term/immediate) financial obligations.

This ratio is calculated by:

$$\frac{\text{Current assets}}{\text{Current liabilities}} : 1$$

For example, if this ratio is 1:1, then current assets equal current liabilities, so your business can pay its way at that moment in time.

If this ratio is less than 1, then cash or near to cash coming into your business is less than cash or near to cash going out: A position which is nonsustainable over the longer term.

The acid test, sometimes known as the quick ratio, gives a truer indication of your business's short-term liquidity. This is because the current assets are adjusted to include only those that are readily turned into cash. This means that stock and inventory are excluded as you look to gain a more accurate measure of your business's ability to meet its short or more immediate financial obligations.

This ratio is calculated by:

$$\frac{\text{Current assets} - \text{stock}}{\text{Current liabilities}} : 1$$

The importance of excluding stock will be relative to the type of business you run. The key aspect is being how quickly your stock can be converted into cash.

For example, if you sell fruit, salad, and vegetables, your stock must be converted (i.e., sold) quickly; otherwise, it will be worthless (being perishable). Alternatively, if you sell cars or vans, it is more likely sales may not be so immediate (i.e., conversion to cash taking much longer).

The long-term solvency of your business will evolve as you become more established. You will then need to consider your gearing ratio. This is when you compare the level of borrowing as a proportion of long-term finance. Most would say the higher the proportion of the former to the latter, the greater the risk of your business failing.

The primary reason for this is that any borrowing needs to be paid for, by interest and possibly charges. So, funds need to be generated via your business's cash flow to facilitate timely payment of these interest payments.

Efficiency Ratios

These ratios are also of vital importance as they indicate how effectively your business manages its stock/inventory, creditors, and debtors. These three financial metrics, as we have seen, are part of your working capital (current assets – current liabilities), measuring your business's liquidity. Therefore, is it critical that they are closely managed and understood.

Stock Turnover

This figure indicates how many times per year your stock is converted into cash. Clearly, the higher the level of stock turnover, the greater benefit to your business's liquidity.

Depending on what your business does, the ideal scenario is to keep stock levels as low as possible. Essentially, any money tied up on stock is idle money and could be put to better use in other areas of your business.

To calculate stock turnover, you need to:

- Calculate your average stock:

$$\frac{\text{Opening stock} + \text{closing stock}}{2}$$

- Then calculate:

$$\frac{\text{Cost of sales}}{\text{Average stock}}$$

- Finally divide this figure into 52 (weeks in the year). Alternatively divide this figure into 365 to give the number of days taken to convert stock to cash.

Creditor Turnover

This figure indicates the speed with which your business adheres to its short-term financial obligations: that is, the number of weeks which your creditors wait for payment.

As your creditors will include your suppliers and the tax authorities, their payments must be thoughtfully monitored and managed.

Late payment to suppliers, for example, may lead to less beneficial terms next time. Perhaps, worse as your suppliers may demand payment on delivery.

We can calculate this metric by:

$$\frac{\text{Cost of sales}}{\text{Average creditors or year} - \text{end creditors}}$$

- Then divide this figure into 52 (weeks in the year). Or, as above, divide this figure into 365 to give the number of days your business takes to pay its creditors.

Debtor Turnover

This figure shows the average rate with which you receive payment for products or services provided: that is, how long your clients take to may payment to you.

This figure is calculated by:

$$\frac{\text{Total sales}}{\text{Average debtors or year} - \text{end debtors}}$$

- Then divide this figure into 52 (weeks in the year). Or alternatively, divide this figure into 365 to reveal the number of days it takes for you to receive payment.

These efficiency ratios are therefore key indicators to enable you to understand your business's propensity to survive and thrive by meeting its financial commitments.

Example of financial statements:

Income statement for the periods ending 1-31-21 and 3-31-22

	2021	2022
	£000	£000
Sales revenue	5,500	7,500
Cost of sales	(1,450)	(1,770)
Gross profit	4,050	5,730
Overheads	(1,280)	(1,400)
Depreciation	(300)	(300)
Operating profit	2,470	4,030
Interest on bank loan	(100)	(100)
Net profit for the period	2,370	3,930

Breakdown of overheads

	£000	£000
Salaries and wages	1,000	1,200
Rates, utility bills, etc.	40	40
Advertising	90	175
Logistics	100	120
Other	50	65
	1,480	1,600

Statement of financial position at 1-31-21 and 3-31-22

	2021	2022
	£000	£000
Assets		
Fixed Assets		
Buildings	830	830
Machines	500	420
Motor vehicles	220	200
	1,550	1,450
Current assets		

Inventory	100	240
Trade receivables	260	260
Cash in the bank	150	180
	510	680
Equity and liability		
Equity		
Shareholder funds	1,000	2,080
Retained profit	280	240
	1,280	2,320
Noncurrent liabilities		
Bank loan	300	300
Current liabilities		
Trade payables	150	150
Tax	180	160
Dividends	240	200
	570	510
Total equity and liabilities	2,150	3,030

Example Ratios

Gross profit as a percent of sales
(Calculated by Gross profit/Sales × 100)

2021:

$$\frac{4,050}{5,500} = 73\%$$

2022:

$$\frac{5,730}{7,500} = 76\%$$

These figures indicate that gross profit as a percent of sales is increasing.

Working capital ratio
(Calculated by Current assets/Current liabilities:1)

2021:

$$\frac{510}{570} : 1 = 0.89 : 1$$

2022:

$$\frac{680}{510} : 1 = 1.33 : 1$$

We can see from these figures that in both years, there is evidence of the ability to meet ongoing financial obligations. In addition, the working capital ratio is improving from 2018 to 2019.

Acid test/liquidity ratio
   (Calculated by Current assets – Inventory/Current liabilities:1)
   2021:

$$\frac{510-100}{570} : 1 = \frac{410}{570} : 1 = 0.72 : 1$$

2022:

$$\frac{680-240}{510} : 1 = \frac{440}{510} : 1 = 0.86 : 1$$

This indicates that the levels of liquidity are improving. This ratio, as inventory is excluded, gives a more accurate indication of the business's ability to meet its ongoing financial commitments.

Stock turnover
   This indicates the frequency in which inventory and stock are converted into cash. The higher the frequency, the greater increase in liquidity.
   Calculated by Cost of sales/Inventory. Then, work out average days taken to convert stock into sales.

2021:

$$\frac{1{,}450}{100} = 14.5 \qquad \frac{365}{14.5} = 25.2$$

2022:

$$\frac{1{,}770}{240} = 7.4 \qquad \frac{365}{7.4} = 49.3$$

We can see from these figures the conversion of inventory/stock to sales increases between 2021 and 2022.

Don't ever let your business get ahead of the financial side of your business. Accounting, accounting, accounting. Know your numbers.
—Tilman J. Fertitta

CHAPTER 10

Managing Expansion

You can never be satisfied as an entrepreneur, and the basis of any successful, growing business is new clients.

—Robert Herjavec

Having gone through the initial start-up and after a certain time period of getting established, it is natural to start to think about expanding your business. Entrepreneurs know that to increase profits and reach new customers, expansion is needed. There are many different ways of doing this, and each approach represents differing levels of risk and challenges. You can follow any and all, depending on your type of business and what level of risk you are willing to take.

As covered in Chapter 3, there are a number of key areas to consider before deciding whether it is the right time or indeed the right decision to pursue expansion. Another useful tool to aid decision making is a SWOT analysis which is covered in Chapter 2.

The Ansoff Matrix is commonly used to identify business growth opportunities. According to the Ansoff Matrix, there are four different strategies to expand your business, each with a various level of risk attached:

- *Market penetration:* This tends to be the safest course to take as you already know the market and products you will be targeting. Finding new customers in an existing market, selling more products to an already established customer, or widening an existing product range can usually be done with little risk or research, but can achieve business growth. This strategy could be considered to be very much "business as usual."
- *Product development:* This is a strategy that aims to introduce new products into existing markets and can be more risky as

there is uncertainty to how a market may react. Successful innovation is important but so are insights into how customers will take to it. A strategy like this could be suitable for businesses where a product can be differentiated for the business to maintain competitiveness.

- *Market development:* The risk extends further here. Going global offers many opportunities. However, with so much choice, there is a risk or decreased focus. Chasing too many opportunities and currency fluctuations can increase risk and lead to pitfalls. This requires a lot of research as there are cultural differences to consider as well as how new customers in overseas markets will take to your product. It is also important to note here that market development does not have to mean globalization; it can mean working a shop 500 miles away in the same country, new product packing or dimensions, new distribution channels, or different pricing policies to create new market segments.

- *Diversification:* The riskiest of the four strategies. This entails going into a new market with new products, with limited chance of using any existing knowledge. Even businesses who have followed this strategy to grow previously can fail when repeating the process, due to the level of "unknowns." For a business to successfully use this strategy, there must be a clear understanding of what it wants to achieve and a clear and honest appraisal of the risks. However, with the right balance of risk and reward, a diversification strategy can be rewarding.

As expected, for many businesses, growth is a signal for success, creating new opportunities, attracting new customers, and as a result increased profit. However, expanding a business is not without risks. Decisions like this should be subject to a SWOT analysis, and the pros and cons should be considered before deciding to pursue growth.

Advantages of Business Growth

One of the greatest competitive advantages of business growth is the ability to capitalize on the economies of scale. In microeconomics, this concept outlines the cost advantage obtained as production output increases. Costs can be both fixed and variable. This means a business can achieve savings in:

- *Purchasing:* By getting discounts for buying in bulk. This is one of the most well-known advantages of economies of scale.
- *Marketing:* By spreading the cost of marketing and promotions over a larger number of sales.
- *Overheads:* By spreading the administrative or staff costs across a greater level of output.

This is an important concept for any business, whatever the industry, and represents the cost advantages large businesses have over the smaller ones. A common question from consumers is why the prices charged in small business are higher than that of a similar item in a larger business. The size of a business is relevant when it comes to economies of scale. The larger the business, the larger the savings. Economies of scale can be both internal and external: Internal are based on decisions by management, while external are based on external factors.

Business growth can also enable you to:

- *Increase stock and resources:* As demand increases, that can put pressures on supply. If a business is in a period of expansion, they may be able to increase supplies of goods and be more prepared for a continually increasing demand and number of customers.
- *Put more money back into your business:* As more money comes in, this can open the door to opportunities to invest. This can be in new facilities, more up-to-date equipment, or staff and areas such as staff training.
- *Influence market prices:* Due to the bulk buying advantages of economies of scale, a larger business may choose to decide to pass those cost savings on to the customer.
- *Increased profile:* A larger or ever-expanding business will attract more attention, certainly locally and regionally and in some cases by the media. This in turn will organically spread

the word and lead to an increased profile for your business. This can organically lead to a higher profile for you as the entrepreneur and potentially open doors to other opportunities outside of the day job.

- *Reach new markets and customers and subsequently increase sales and profits:* A larger business can be more equipped to deal with importing and exporting and reaching markets abroad. This can be a complex, and bureaucratic area, research, and hiring well is key.
- *Reduce external risks:* For example, from competitors or technology and market changes.
- *Add new talent to your business:* This can include hiring new members of staff on a permanent or temporary basis or consulting with outside expertise. One of the key decisions here is to consider whether permanent full-time staff are needed, part-time staff are needed, or whether it is better to take on contractors or outsource parts of your operation.
  A decision like this will largely depend on the type of business and the type of operation, particularly if busy times come in peaks and troughs or if some elements (such as web design or accounting) need some external expertise. Each type or category of new employee will have certain pros and cons, but it is worth remembering that if you take on employee's, they are your responsibility and it is important to treat them fairly—that means being familiar with areas such as annual leave allowances, absence, and a fair reward and retention strategy.
- *Share responsibility:* As you expand, there is likely to be more business areas or departments and people to manage. This may mean that management, leadership, and responsibility have to be shared out. When going through this process, experience in dealing with areas such as recruitment, payroll, and HR is likely to be needed at some stage. It is important to ensure that the advice you get in this area is of a high quality as there are legal and moral responsibilities here. While there

will be some increased costs for "doing it properly," the costs of not are potentially much greater, in terms of potential staff churn, low moral possibly leading to lower productivity, and the reputational damage if your business is highlighted as one that does not care about its employees.

With expansion and adding talent comes the need for teamwork and the need to a positive workplace culture. A "high-performance work team" could be defined as goal-focused individuals, bringing specialized skills and expertise, working together to deliver consistently superior outputs and results.

There are some key principles to consider and follow when it comes to building a high-performing team and characteristics of a high-performance culture. This will be a balancing act in some cases, but broadly speaking, it is a case of doing simple things, consistently well. High-performing teams:

- Communicate regularly, respectfully, and clearly
- Have clearly defined roles and responsibilities
- Respect and trust each other
- Practice ongoing learning and self-development
- Manage workload and deadlines based on priorities
- Recognize contributions and celebrate achievement and success together—always make time to do this
- Understand how their work fits into the overriding organizational mission
- Have clearly defined goals, which are closely tied to the team and organizational priorities

Company culture is also a crucial concept as it correlates to team performance and company revenues. Culture is not just values or engagement; it is about business goals, social impact, and driving change. Key components of company culture are clear vision and strategic direction, values, teamwork, buy in from all stakeholders, communication, social impact and diversity, and inclusion.

Potential Disadvantages of Business Growth

As a business expands, by definition the business model will become more complex. This is by no means insurmountable, and isn't a reason not to pursue expansion, but it can increase the likelihood of potential pitfalls as you proceed. Being aware of how these apply to your business is critical, and as with many other aspects of entrepreneurship, awareness and preparation will undoubtedly help with mitigating problems that arise. Some common issues with business expansion include the following:

- *Cash flow shortages:* With the costs of expansion and the potential for unexpected costs, there may be a need to borrow cash to fund expansion. For example, paying for new premises or equipment. With added assets or premises, will come additional costs.
- *Compromised quality:* An increase in production output may lead to a decline in quality of goods produced due to increased margin for error. This can lead to a loss of sales and customers.
- *Loss of control:* As you expand your business, hire new staff, and put management teams in place, you may need to delegate duties or share workloads. This will organically lead to some loss of control, which can be unsettling in the short term—particularly, if you started the business as a one-person operation. Good recruitment and strong leadership skills are key areas to consider here. If this is in place and is of a good quality, then the risk of issues, such as poorly outsourced recruitment, poor staff retention, or not finding the best candidates for key positions, can be minimized.
- *Increased capital requirements:* A bigger business or a business that is increasingly expanding will at some point need more staff, more or larger premises, more equipment (or a mixture of all), and as a result, more investment of capital. Again, keeping a regular eye on your numbers is vital, investing for growth is okay, but losing oversight and control of your finances is not.

- *Increased responsibility for new areas:* With expansion comes new responsibility. This can potentially be areas that any entrepreneur may be unfamiliar with. This can be areas such as HR, staff absence, payroll, and more complex accounting procedures being needed.
- *Staff turnover:* As workloads increase, staff morale could drop, productivity could drop, and in some cases that can lead to staff deciding to leave. Another possibility is of having to dismiss staff, which is where knowledge of relevant legislation comes in. Staff leaving means having to spend time and money replacing them and ensuring you find the right fit for the roles you need to fill. Having a staff retention policy in place can be helpful here. Having a positive culture and reward and recognition for high performers is likely to increase the chances of staff loyalty.

It is important here to recognize that expansion can be disruptive. It can, and is likely to, affect every part of your business and can pressurize staff, finances, and resources. This is why expansion needs to be planned carefully in a measured and informed way.

Balance is really important here. However, if you make a well-researched, balanced choice, your business is given the best possible opportunity to continue to thrive.

Starting and growing a business is as much about the innovation, drive, and determination of the people behind it as the product they sell.

—Elon Musk

CHAPTER 11

Understanding Resources

There is one and only one responsibility of business; to use its resources and engage in activities designed to increase its profits so as it stays within the rules of the game.

—Milton Friedman

In this chapter, many of the themes discussed elsewhere will align. Understanding your perspectives of resourcing and resource management is critical to running a successful business and building a solid platform for growth and expansions. A great deal of the principles discussed will be applicable throughout the entrepreneurial journey, irrespective of business type or size.

As a series of start points:

- Make sure you understand yourself—have a clear self-understanding of why you want to embark on your entrepreneurial adventures. For example, you may consider your current and aspirational skills and competencies, your areas of expertise, your aims and desired outcomes, and your hoped-for work–life balance. Entrepreneurship will mean that every part of your life will change; you need to maximize the chances of everything working out well for you and other stakeholders, including family and employees. Ongoing self-awareness is essential.
- *You need to have an idea, your idea:* This idea will fortify every aspect of your business. Your idea and your vision for your business make you different and unique from your competitors. Ultimately, your idea justifies the reason for your business's existence and provides a platform to build on.

- *Your dedication and drive are crucial:* For many entrepreneurs, especially in the early stages, long hours and some erratic working schedules are the norm. This commitment, your commitment, requires your time and ultimately sacrifice. You will also need to support and understanding of your family and friends.

- *Expertise, possibly from a range of sources, is usually essential, especially in your early days:* Advice may be sought for the legal, finance, and marketing strategies of your business. Critical issues to consider include your business name, registration of your business, any required permits to trade, trademarks, copyrights and patents, obtaining a license, and opening a business bank account. As you go through any period of expansion, expertise in trading outside domestic markets, HR, and employment law may need to be sought.

- *There is a need to plan, for the short, medium, and long term (this is covered in more detail in Chapter 6):* Your business plan is a document that will continually be appraised and need to continually evolve. To retain its value and to have meaning, your business plan needs to be regularly reviewed and updated to accommodate inevitable internal and external changes.

- *How you will structure your business:* For example, will you be a sole trader, set up a partnership, or set up a limited company. This may well be an area where professional advice will prove invaluable. This is an area to keep under review, some business models lend themselves to certain types and size of business, and if you are planning or going through expansion, your structure may need to change.

- *Your business needs capital:* Your capital is your acquisition or access to various sources of funds, that is, money in the bank (liquid funds) or money you can access. As has been referred to in previous chapters, there are many sources of funds, including your own savings (bootstrapping), grants, loans, private investor finance, crowdfunding, or family.

- *You need a place to work, a suitable venue that is commensurate with the stage of evolution of your business:* Your workplace needs to be appropriate with your type of business, your image, and brand. Your place of work also needs to be accessible to your customers, employees, colleagues, and any other stakeholders. Accessibility can of course be face to face and/or via technology.

In the early days of your business, and as a good practice dictates, every day after, cost awareness and control must be a top a priority. So, if you are seeking premises, find out the rental costs, the utilities, and other costs before committing. Also be careful of any other costs you may occur and keep this area under review.

- You need to have something to sell—your product or service offering. So, research, design, production, packaging, market testing, distribution, and legal compliance are some of the key stages of your entrepreneurial journey. Quite possibly you will need to source expertise, guidance, or a second opinion along the way.
- Depending on your scale of operations, you may need to build a team—perhaps, an employee, a business partner, or freelancer. When building your team, it is really important to establish a shared vision, clear goals, and clarity of roles and responsibilities. Involving others also offers you the opportunity to build your business culture and sets a foundation to build on in terms of adding new employees. If a vision and culture is already established, it will be more straightforward to add new employees to your business.
- *You need customers:* No customers mean no business. Your marketing strategies are therefore another key component of your success. Ultimately, your business's future and very survival depends on its ability to generate sales and income.

Over time, when all goes to plan, your business will prosper and potentially grow. Today, your effective use of social media is crucial as is your (internal and external) customer service. You need to be prepared to compete in an ever more uncertain and volatile marketplace and business environment.

- *Embracing feedback from all directions adds immeasurable value:* Invite ideas, involve others, and seek opinion that may in some cases be different to your own. Often, a different perspective can lead to a better outcome. Ultimately, all stakeholders will have views and listening and being receptive will serve you well. This is also an approach that can gain you brand advocates, people who will spread the positive message about your product and service offering. Also remember that negative feedback can also be extremely valuable. Those offering such comments may well be trying to be helpful; furthermore, they may have a very valid opinion that is worthy of your time to consider further.

Understanding the People Resource

As you go through the entrepreneurial journey, there may well be a time where you have to think about hiring new staff. This may be from the beginning or in some cases as you go through a period of growth or expansion.

It is important to note that this can be an advantage to your business as it either leads to expanding the knowledge and skillset available or simply means that you need more people to meet demand. However, it also comes with great responsibility. As an employer, there are a number of areas to consider such as holidays and sick leave, and as an entrepreneur, the success of your business is relied upon by both you and your employees. Ultimately, if there is a success, you all share that success, but if things go off track, the business potentially closes, and there is potential for a large amount of people who lose their jobs. So, this is not an area to be taken lightly.

In terms of deciding whether to hire, it will largely depend on what type of work you need help with, and whether it is a seasonal type of work or something more permanent. This will largely depend on the type of business and the quantity of demand. But this is an important consideration, and you don't want to hire full-time staff for three- to four-month demand and end up with employees with nothing to do.

It is also important when hiring to be really clear about what type of person you are looking for—not just in terms of qualifications and experience but also in terms of character and whether they will fit into your company culture. This is an important concept to consider in terms of staff retention. If you have a positive culture that encourages participation and opportunities for development as well as having a fair and transparent reward and recognition strategy, employees will be more likely to stay (or at least less likely to be actively looking to leave).

As you expand, it may be a consideration to put management teams in place for parts of the business. This may be due to increased volumes of demand or because specialist support is needed in certain areas. An example of this could be hiring a marketing or social media expert to head a team in that area. Another example could be hiring a HR expert to manage areas such as staff welfare. This can be beneficial, particularly if you are adding expertise and filling a skills gap in your team. However, in the early days, usually a team is relatively small (potentially one or two people), so there must also be a realization that if you add levels of management, there will be increased ideas and input and also a dilution of the entrepreneur's level of control. This can work both ways, but it is important to do your research and ensure you are getting good-quality people that you can trust and give that you are comfortable to give level of responsibility.

However, it is important to note that being an employer means added responsibility for payroll, annual leave, sickness and absence, health and safety, and various other aspects of employment law. Irrespective of management teams or how you divide business areas, the entrepreneur has overall responsibility. These areas will have an impact on your business in one way or another and must be taken seriously.

In conclusion, during this brief chapter, we have tried to collate a range of themes discussed elsewhere in more detail. One of the primary purposes is to try and demonstrate how so many different actions need to be adeptly and consistently aligned when you look for entrepreneurial success. Any business, of any size, will run a lot more smoothly when the various, and sometimes many, moving parts run together in an efficient way.

You need a relentless drive that others may not have to give yourself a maximum chance of success. Your vision will inspire you and your key stakeholders. Your business needs a clear, yet adaptable strategic vision and you need to pay attention to every single detail. Importantly, you will have a willingness to continually learn, to continually improve, to self-develop, and to inspire the same for those around you.

> *I've learned, like with anything else, business is only as good as your connections and your resources. And some of the resources that I have are the fact that I work with huge artists.*
>
> —Daymond John

CHAPTER 12

Process Management

The whole idea of process management is; the chain of actions to be made effective and efficient.

—Hans van Krevel

In any type of business, there will be numerous processes to manage to ensure efficient running, some of these areas will be relevant from the beginning, others may become important as the business grows, and some may be important depending on the size and type of business. Whatever the circumstances, there are numerous important areas that will need consideration and research as you embark on your entrepreneurial journey.

Taxation

In the early stages of setting up, running, or establishing your business, you may consider seeking the advice of an accountant or tax adviser (this is usually a good idea, particularly if the domestic tax rules or the tax rules with countries you trade with are complex). You can then obtain professional advice on your tax position to ensure you pay your relevant and correct tax obligations on time. While this type of specialist support will come at a monetary cost, it pays to start this process properly. And unless you are a trained accountant, it may well be both more time and cost efficient to have this type of support from the beginning as any mistakes or miscalculations can be potentially costly and problematic.

As an entrepreneur, it is your responsibility to be aware of the tax implications, together with any changes, for your business.

Income Tax

Everyone pays income tax. If you are a sole trader and self-employed, you may well carry out a tax self-assessment. If you have set up a company (which as mentioned in Chapter 2 is a separate legal entity), you will be an employee of your company, so your income tax will be collected via the PAYE system.

If you are self-employed, income tax is payable on the profits of your business. This is because it is taken as personal income as there is no legal separation of your personal and business income. However, as the profit or loss for your business activities cannot be predicted, the income tax is due retrospectively, in almost all cases as a single payment.

In the United States as in the United Kingdom, income is taxed by Federal/Central Government. In the United States, state and local governments are also involved. Both tax systems are progressive, so the rate of taxation increases as income increases.

However, if your business is a limited company, you are likely to draw a salary which means the tax authorities consider you as an employee of the business. You may decide not to draw a salary, instead you may pay yourself a dividend at the end of your financial year. Either way, you have an income tax liability if your total income exceeds your current personal allowances (i.e., the amount you can earn tax free).

Corporation Tax

This is the tax your company pays on its profits. Generally, your business decides how much corporation tax it owes and is calculated via a self-assessment process. This tax is calculated at the end of every financial year and must be paid within the stated timescales to the tax authorities in the United States to the Internal Revenue Service (IRS) and in the United Kingdom to Her Majesty's Revenue and Customs (HMRC).

Corporation tax is imposed in the United States at the federal, most state, and many local levels on the declared income of all businesses.

All bills, invoices, and receipts must be kept for five years after submitting a corporation tax return, so that you can verify, and figures should the tax authorities decide to seek clarity.

You can normally claim for a range of business expenses, and these can include the following:

- All costs incurred for the sole purpose of generating business profits
- The cost of goods for resale and the costs of raw materials

- Wages and salaries, employer's National Insurance (NI) contributions (see below), insurance costs, and pension benefits
- Costs relating to your dedicated business premises, for example, heating lighting, water rates, and business rates. If you work from home, then a quantity of these costs can be claimed
- General maintenance of your business premises (again a proportion if you work from home) and repairs to any business equipment
- Telephone/mobile bills (those calls exclusively for business purposes), postage, stationary, printing, and software
- The running costs of your own vehicle that are attributable to your business. This will include insurance, servicing, repairs, tax, and fuel
- Travel and accommodation on business trips
- Accountant's fees and possibly solicitor's fees
- Special clothing that is exclusively for work purposes

As ever, seeking the advice of an accountant or the tax authorities is certainly worth doing and will be invaluable.

National Insurance (NI)

In the United Kingdom, everyone pays NI. There are different rates for employees and the self-employed. If you become an employer (see later in this chapter), you have the responsibility to collect and pay the NI for your employees. The self-employed do this themselves.

Currently, there are four categories of NI.

Class 1: This is where employers pay NI contributions for most of their employees, including directors, part-timers, and contract workers. There are a few exceptions: for example, employees who are under 16 or those who earn below a certain threshold.

Class 2: This applies if you are self-employed although you can be exempt if you are making below the current threshold.

Class 3: This is a voluntary rate paid by individuals who want to fill any gaps in their contributions record.

Class 4: As with Class 2, this applies if you are self-employed and it levied on your annual profits. This tax is collected concurrently with your income tax.

In the United States, there is provision for health insurance, which offers a range of options that help pay for medical expenses, whether privately purchased or obtained via social insurance or a government-funded social welfare program.

Value-Added Tax (VAT)

Legally, if you have set up as a company in the United Kingdom, when your annual sales reach the threshold specified by the tax authorities, you are obliged to register for VAT. This tax is usually payable on your sales, so it needs to be added to your invoices. However, you can claim back or offset the VAT on items you purchase for your business.

You can voluntarily register for VAT if you feel it is feasible to do so, that is, the advantages (your ability to recover VAT) against the disadvantages (the need to charge VAT and the additional process costs).

Today, there are several software packages available that will self-generate your VAT and other tax returns. However, it is always important to retain the supporting documentation/records should the tax authorities request sight.

In the United States, there is a system of sales tax that is levied at the state rather than federal level. Most states opt to charge a sales tax although there are considerable variances. However, sales tax is currently not added onto goods and services that are exported from the United States to the United Kingdom.

Capital Gains Tax (CGT)

If you sell something for more than you paid for it, you may be liable for CGT, for example, if you sell a property or another type of investment as an integral aspect of your business activities.

In the United States, short-term capital gains are taxed at the same rate as tax on ordinary income. Long-term capital gains are currently taxed at lower rates.

Minimizing Your Taxable Profits

There are several ways for you to reduce your tax liability. (It always needs to be done in an acceptable and legal way.) If in doubt, seek advice from your accountant or the tax authorities.

Options include:

- If your spouse works with you, they are paid for the work that they undertake.
- If you are self-employed and make a loss in your first year, you can offset that against income from previous years. In these circumstances, you may be entitled to a tax rebate.
- Any self-employed trading losses in any year can be carried forward to offset against future profits from the same trade.
- If you are self-employed, you can also set off any losses against other income received in the same tax year, for example, from private investments.
- If you are set up as a limited company, any trading losses can be offset against other income in the same tax year.
- Payments into a pension scheme can be offset against taxable profits. However, remember that pension contributions are usually inaccessible, so would not be available for use in your business in case of need.
- Log all your allowable expenses. The golden rule is that business costs are allowable, personal costs are not.
- Ensure you claim all the available capital allowances. For example, if you are purchasing office goods, in this case, you can write off a percentage of the value of these assets against profits over several years.

Becoming an Employer

As your business evolves and hopefully goes from strength to strength, maybe sooner rather than later, you may need some external help and may look to take on new employees. In fact, in some cases, you may be working with others from Day 1.

Your primary options are likely to be employing someone or outsourcing a part of your activities to a contractor or to another company.

Employing someone obviously costs money; however, you should regard this eventuality as a key investment from your business. However, you must remember, when you employ someone, you have a series of very important legal obligations, for example, taxation and working conditions.

Recruitment

There are so many exciting times when starting your own business, with a considerable range of things to think about. In the early phases, you may be working alone as you look to get established. However, at some stage, possibly from the outset, you may need to have support from others.

Recruiting may be a new experience for you, so here are several issues you need to consider:

- Do you need to recruit? Is it essential? Can your business support it and are you truly ready to be an employer?
- Why do you want to recruit? Your rationale needs to be crystal clear with a specific need and purpose.
- What will be the job content? What will be involved, in terms of the key roles and responsibilities? Is this clear from the outset?
- What terms and conditions will you offer? For example, full-time or part-time (see the following).
- What qualifications and experience will you expect your employee to bring and subsequently contribute to your business's success? Be specific here and try as far as possible to stick to your criteria, even if that is the more time-consuming route. In most cases, it is better to wait for the right person than to rush and get someone who isn't a great fit (a possible "lose lose" situation).
- How will your new employee integrate into your business? In the interests of team spirit and having a great workplace culture, as previously mentioned, getting the right person is paramount.
- The terms and conditions, including salary and any other reward and recognition, that are to be offered.

You have your own network of possible employees, which can also be effective.

Other possible avenues for finding potential employees include the following:

- Job centers, whose primary purpose is to get people into work
- Job seeker and recruitment sites, where you can place an advert on the site for a fee
- Recruitment agencies, which can be a considerable expense in your early days
- Recruitment advertising, largely via social media but can be via local newspapers
- Via your own advertising, website, or newsletter
- Using word of mouth or your own network

If and when you recruit, it is critical for your business that you make the right decision. It is essential that you recruit the right person, for the right reasons at the right time.

One major risk is if you recruit on gut feeling on instinct. This may work well because you will probably be working closely with your colleague, and you need to get on well with them. With that said, ultimately you need your employees to make an effective contribution to your business's success. It is also worth noting that employees have rights, and if you make the wrong choice, you may end up having to make the best of it.

Types of Employees

Permanent employees: A full-time employee has a contract with you without a time limit on it, that is, open-ended. A full-time employee usually implies they will offer a normal working week (as defined and agreed in the contract of work).

Part-time employees: They also have an open-ended contract of employment, expect this will be for fewer hours or less days than a full-time employee. Again, the exact details will be clarified in the contract of work.

Fixed-term contracts: This would be where you take on an employee with a contractual arrangement that has a specific finish date (this may be a date or when a specific job, task, or defined time period has been completed).

NB: For both permanent and part-time employees, your employer obligations are the same, for example, in terms of pay and conditions, any benefits package and pension provisions.

Temporary employees: These employees would usually be supplied via an employment agency. Your contract, therefore, is with the employment agency rather than the employee.

Freelancers, consultants, and contractors: Each of these categories are self-employed, effectively independent businesses selling their skills and services to you. Any agreement between you and them is always best formalized, probably by a contract. This means you and they are clear about the terms and conditions services are to be provided. These types of employees are responsible for their own tax liabilities.

Your obligations for permanent employees include the following:

- Providing a written contract of employment
- Offer a minimum level of paid holiday and a maximum working week (as specified in the contract of employment)
- Paying your employees at least the minimum wage (e.g., set by the U.S. labor law and a range of state and local laws or in the United Kingdom by Central Government)
- Provide an itemized pay statement
- Registering all employees with the tax authorities (in the United States by the IRS and in the United Kingdom via the HMRC)
- Provide a safe and secure working environment
- Taking out the appropriate insurance cover to protect all parties (including you) against claims for illness or injury
- Possibly offer statutory sick pay. The specifics of your obligations will vary from country to county. For example, in the United States, there is no national requirement to offer paid sick leave, although many states have their own laws

- Treating all your employees fairly, avoiding discrimination
- Following the correct procedures if there was a need to dismiss an employee or make them redundant

Paying Your Employees

All employees aged 18 or over are legally entitled to be paid at least the minimum wage (as mentioned earlier).

The different options to pay employees include the following:

- *Salary:* This is where your employee(s) are on a fixed salary where a specific annual figure is earned. Payment frequencies are usually monthly or weekly. The figure paid to your employee will normally be net of any tax and, if appropriate (dependent on local country legislation), insurance.
- *Hourly rate:* Here, your employees will receive a specific amount (pretax) for each hour of work. The number of hours may be specified by contractual arrangement, and often, there is a minimum expectation for hours worked. Overtime rates may apply if you ask your employee to work additional hours. From your perspective, this approach has the advantage of you only paying your employees for the hours required. Your employees may feel this option gives them greater flexibility although possibly less job security.
- *Commission:* This scheme means your employee is paid solely on performance or output/productivity, for example, an agreed percentage per sale, or payment upon meeting an agreed target. The benefit of this approach for you is that your employees are paid (therefore incentivized) by results. So, you and they benefit if targets are met or even better, exceeded. However, from your employee's view, there is inevitable uncertainty about whether they will do enough to achieve their targets. Their ability to do so may well be influenced by a range of factors outside their control.

The Tax Position of Your Employees

When you take on an employee, you have legal obligations requiring their income text and possibly (depending on your global location) NI contributions.

An employee:

- Is Anyone you employ under a contract of service, whether explicit (documented) or clearly implied
- Included here are directors, business partners, part-time employees, or casual workers

NB: An employee usually doesn't include those who are self-employed. In the event of doubt, clarity can be obtained from the tax authorities. This will be, for example, the Internal Revenue Service in the United States and the HMRC in the United Kingdom.

As soon as you become an employer, you need to register with the tax authorities.

You will need to keep a payroll, which calculates how much pay is due to each employee, together with the amount of tax and, if appropriate, NI that is payable.

In the United States, usually some form of employee insurance/protection is compulsory. In many states, there is Part 1 for compulsory coverages and Part 2 for noncompulsory coverage. Essentially employee compensation is structured as an insurance system, where any wage and medical costs are financed via insurance premiums.

Employment Law

Employment law is becoming ever more extensive and complex and is continually changed and updated.

In the United States, under the Fair Labor Standards Act, employers are required to:

- Pay the minimum wage
- Pay overtime for hours worked more than 40 hours per week
- There are many local state laws regarding minimum wage, overtime, and mandatory breaks

In the United States, the most important federal employment laws you need to embrace, once you become an employer, are as follows:

- Job discrimination
- Overtime/minimum wage
- Family leave
- Age discrimination
- Disability discrimination
- Military leave
- Gender-pay alignment
- Workplace safety

Likewise, in the United Kingdom, employment legislation will place obligations on you as an employee, in several sensitive areas including those given as follows:

- Minimum wage
- Discrimination based on trade union membership
- Working time directive
- Disability discrimination
- Discrimination based on race, gender and faith
- Equal pay for equal work

Discrimination

As an employer, there are two forms of discrimination you must be aware of:

- *Direct discrimination:* Usually, this is clear enough to see and therefore avoid. This is where you would openly treat one sector of the community less favorably than others. Most direct discrimination is explicitly against the law. For example, if you are looking to recruit and say only a certain gender can apply or if you were to refrain from interviewing potential employees in the basis of their color, religion, or origin.
- *Indirect discrimination:* Often, this is a more contentious area, although in the event of any dispute, often the tendency is

to favor the complainant rather than the employer. Indirect discrimination is where you are shown to place an unnecessary requirement or condition on a particular job you are recruiting for which will, by clear implication, exclude certain members of the community. An example would be a requirement for fluent English when the role doesn't require such a skill.

Quite clearly, good working relationship with all your employees is a fundamental characteristic of good business practice. There is also good reason to avoid any issues of discrimination. First, if any cases are proven against you, there will be compensation implications. Furthermore, there could be considerable reputational damage.

Disciplinary Procedures

In this area, any rules must be fair, proportionate, and reasonable.
   Typically, rules will include:

- Work performance
- Expectations around productivity, timekeeping, and absenteeism
- Negligence and disregard for safety or hygiene regulations
- Theft, including fraud
- Offensive behavior, including abuse, harassment, discrimination, and violence
- Inappropriate behavior, including misuse of company facilities

Employer Liability

If you employ anyone, in most cases, you are legally obliged to have employer's liability insurance. This is a policy that protects you from any compensation and legal costs that result from claims that employees may make who are injured/made ill as a result of their employment with you.
   In the United States, if you employ an American national, you must take out the American equivalent of Employer's Liability to comply with

local law. Furthermore, if you are employing an American national, they will not be covered by a British employer's liability insurance policy. All your employees will be required to have a U.S. Federal ID Number.

Health and Safety

An integral aspect of entrepreneurship is managing risk. Every business will face risks, especially in the early days, for example, with cash flow and bad debts.

It is vital to remember that in the unfortunate circumstances of a serious accident to you or an employee, you could be put out of business.

Ensuring your place of work is safe is a legal requirement, and there are penalties (in some cases they can be severe) for noncompliance.

In the United States, the Department of Labor (DOL) has responsibility for the administration and enforcement of the prevailing health and safety legislation. All employers, obviously including you, have a general duty to provide work and a workplace free from recognized and serious hazards (as stated in the Occupational Safety and Health Act 1970).

In the United Kingdom, the Health and Safety and Work Act 1974 (HASAWA) determines a wide range of responsibilities for employer's adherence. You as employer are legally required to protect the health, safety, and welfare of all your employees, as well as any others, while on your premises. This requirement includes temps, casual workers, self-employed, clients, visitors, and the public.

Managing Your Cash Flow

Most would say that your cash flow is the lifeblood of your business. So, it is critical that you receive and make payments on time. You need to ensure that you get paid on time so (via cash or near to cash) you have the means to finance your ongoing/day-to-day financial commitments.

Planning for Prompt Payment

There are several aspects that need to be explained to your customers before confirming an order.

These include the following:

- *Your credit period:* How long you are prepared to wait for payment. The process here is for you to raise an invoice which then passes through your customer's systems, and if appropriate, approval processes before payment to you is confirmed. There is a real-world risk that your customer will delay payment as long as possible as this is best for their own cash flow. Thirty days from the date of your invoice is the common credit period. For a brand-new customer, which all of yours will be in your early stages, you may offer no credit period at all, until your business relationship becomes more established and secure.
- *Carriage charges:* If you are selling goods rather than services, then any carriage or dispatch costs need to be included in your invoice.
- *Additional expenses:* If you are selling services, you may incur additional expenses, which need to be defined, clarified, and agreed with your customer, for example, travel and accommodation costs.
- *Retention of title clause:* These can be included in your invoice, depending on what you are selling, most likely goods. This means the goods remain your property until paid for.

Validation of Your Customer's Creditworthiness

Clearly, it is important that you are comfortable with your customer's ability to pay you the agreed amount on time.

There are a range of details you need to acquire:

- Identification of your customer although in some instances they may already be known to you
- Full name and address
- Contact details for any payment queries, including address, telephone/mobile numbers, and e-mail

- Address to send invoices if different from the aforementioned
- Your customer's banking details

Hopefully, everything will go to plan when you invoice, that is, you receive prompt payment. However, the real world tells us it is always best to be prepared for all eventualities.

Your Invoices

Your invoices should be clear and easy to comprehend.

They should include the following:

- The amount due
- An exact description of the goods or services provided
- Your customers purchase order or reference number. It is essential to have a clear audit trail
- Your terms and conditions
- Date for payment (based on the credit period confirmed in your terms and conditions)
- Your address and contact details
- Your VAT number, if applicable
- Your bank details: name, account number, and sort code

Always be prompt with your invoicing. Send your invoices out the day your goods are delivered or services provided. As above, ensure your invoice goes to the correct contact (this is particularly important when dealing with a larger organization).

Chasing Payments

This may be an experience you will never encounter. However, it is always best to be prepared.

If payment becomes overdue, send a prompt reminder. NB: A payment is defined as late if it has not been made by the last day of the agreed credit period.

Hopefully, any late payments will be due to a genuine oversight by your customer.

In case of need, you may need to:

- Contact your customer by phone
- Send your customer a letter of claim, which can be sent any time after an invoice becomes overdue. This is a letter putting your customer on notice that court proceedings may be brought against them
- Commence legal proceedings (further details on the legal aspects are beyond the scope of this book)

As with previous chapters, this chapter has looked to bring together many different aspects of running a business. There is always a lot to consider and to balance, but with tenacity and a willingness to learn, comes a foundation for success.

We should work on our process, not the outcome of our processes.
—W. Edwards Deming

CHAPTER 13

Trading in Other Countries and Trading Blocs

One of the most underestimated opportunities for developing countries is trade facilitation.

—Karrien Van Gennip

At the early stages of starting and establishing a business, entrepreneurs tend to focus on selling their goods and services in the domestic markets. This is a significant step in "proving the concept" and can then be used as a springboard to look at exploring the international markets. It is important to note that this is another area where there is a lot to consider before deciding whether to pursue international trade and how you may best approach it. There are many opportunities and potential pitfalls in this area of entrepreneurship. So, it requires a great deal of research, and it is best to stay away from bland sayings such as "I only need to sell to 1 percent of the market to make it worthwhile." Sayings like this mean very little and even the "only 1 percent" will likely mean a lot of time and resource and a lot of work to make it happen successfully.

Trading internationally can be an enlightening and positive experience and have benefits for your business. However, it can also be complicated and bureaucratic in some cases. International trade can be defined as allowing countries to expand their markets to access products or services that may not have been available in the domestic markets. For countries and governments that are in favor of international trade, it can be said that this is beneficial and makes markets more competitive.

International trade was an important part in the establishment of the global economy. In the global economy, supply and demand, and as a result prices, both impact and are impacted by global events. For example, political change in Asia could result in an increase in the cost of labor.

This could increase manufacturing costs for a clothing company based in Malaysia. This could then increase the purchase price of a t-shirt in shops in America. So the knock on effects of a particular change can be wide ranging.

Being able to trade between countries can potentially be easier if your domestic country is part of a trading bloc. A trading bloc is usually a group of countries in specific regions that manage and promote trading activities. This leads to liberalization of trade (this is the freedom of trade from protectionist measures) and creation of trade between members. The underlying principle being that member countries are treated favorably in comparison to nonmembers.

The World Trade Organization (WTO) allows the existence of trading blocs on the condition that they provide for lower protection against outside countries than existed before the creation of the trading bloc.

There are several trading blocs. The most significant are as follows:

- *The European Union (EU):* This is made up of a single market, single currency, and a customs union. The EU has 27 European member states and is a unique economic and political union that covers much of the continent. The original creation was the European Economic Community (EEC) in 1958 and what began as a purely economic arrangement now spans policy areas such as health, climate, environment, migration, justice, and security.
- *The European Free Trade Area (EFTA):* This is an intergovernmental organization which was established in 1960 by the EFTA convention. This was to promote economic integration and free trade between member states (Switzerland, Iceland, Norway, and Liechtenstein) both within Europe and globally. Unlike the EU, EFTA does not foresee political integration and does not issue legislation or have a customs union.
- *North American Free Trade Area (NAFTA):* This trade agreement between United States, Mexico, and Canada was signed in 1992 and eventually eliminated all trade barriers and tariffs between member states. This agreement was replaced in 2020 by USMCA which was viewed as a new agreement that

encompassed much of NAFTA but included some significant renegotiations and changes, with a key change coming in the area of automobile manufacture.

- *Mercosur:* A customs union between Brazil, Argentina, Paraguay, Uruguay, and Venezuela. Since its creation, the main objective has been to create a space where investment and business opportunities are generated through competitive integration of national economies into the international market.
- *Association of Southeast Asia Nations (ASEAN):* Established in 1967, by the founding fathers of ASEAN: Malaysia, The Philippines, Indonesia, Thailand, and Singapore. Key aims include to accelerate economic growth between regions, to promote regional peace and collaboration, and to promote Southeast Asian studies.
- *Common Market of Eastern and Southern Africa (COMESA):* Formed in 1994, the main focus of COMESA is on the establishing of a large trading and economic unit that is capable of overcoming some of the barriers that its 21 member states are facing. COMESA priority areas are on a free trade area, a customs union, and trade liberalization and promotion.
- *South Asian Free Trade Area (SAFTA):* Established in 2006, between member countries: Afghanistan, Bangladesh, Sri Lanka, India, Bhutan, Nepal, Maldives, and Pakistan. This is a free trade agreement with a focus on trade liberalization.
- *Pacific Alliance:* Established in 2011, this is a regional trade area between Mexico, Chile, Columbia, and Peru and views itself as a strategic platform that is open to free trade.

It is also important to note that your home country may be a member of more than one trading bloc and may have separate individual arrangements or trade agreements with other countries. This is an important point and one that must be thoroughly checked before making an overall decision about whether to proceed.

Arrangements within trading blocs can change due to internal and external factors. One of the largest recent changes to a trading bloc came when the United Kingdom voted to leave the EU following a referendum. While it is beyond the scope of this book to cover "Brexit" in vast detail or to cover the many differing political and economic viewpoints, it is important to illustrate the impact the period of negotiation had on in business in terms of uncertainty and planning. Following a referendum and the UK voting to leave the EU in 2016, many years of negotiations followed until the eventual full departure on January 1, 2021. This was a complex negotiation, which at times threatened to turn bitter, and the eventual free trade agreement was not fully agreed by the United Kingdom and the EU until December 24, 2021. And even now, there are still areas that have to be negotiated decisions still need to be made on data sharing and financial services, and the agreement on fisheries only lasts five years. There is also the issue of the border between the Republic of Ireland and Northern Ireland, which has still not been fully resolved. In terms of rules, the United Kingdom and the EU have agreed to some identical rules; however, they do not have to be identical in the future, so if one side decides to change that can trigger a dispute and that in turn could lead to tariffs being introduced as punishment.

During this time period, many different plans for Brexit were proposed from each side, with stringent (and it could be argued sometimes idealistic and politically motivated) negotiating positions being taken.

With areas such as tariffs, movement of people and product standards (among many other things) on the table, and the length of time taken for discussions, businesses, both from the United Kingdom and the EU, through no real fault of their own, faced enormous uncertainty and as a result issues with forward planning. This is likely to continue as both parties seek resolution to outstanding issues. But businesses still have to operate and continue to trade as efficiently as they can while this process is ongoing. This affects businesses not only in the United Kingdom and the EU but also in countries who have arrangements with the EU and who seek to continue trading on satisfactory terms with the United Kingdom after Brexit.

Prior to the 2016 referendum, the polling and most opinion strongly suggested that the United Kingdom would vote to remain in the EU.

Subsequent negotiations were only due to last for two years. Both predictions have since been proven to be incorrect.

Regarding Brexit, it is fair to conclude that while this is an extreme example of how things can unexpectedly change, it is also fair to say that expecting the unexpected is an important aptitude to have in this particular area of entrepreneurship.

This also raises the point of ability to negotiate. Being able to negotiate is an important aspect of running in a business and is relevant in a lot of areas. Nevertheless, it is very likely to be needed if you decide to trade overseas. An example of this could be negotiating a bulk buying rate with an outsourcing company to manufacture your product.

In many business scenarios, being able to negotiate and see what you can give the other party without giving away what you don't want to is a vital but sometimes tricky skill to master. Ultimately, being able to negotiate is a critical part of business success. Being well prepared, having a strategy, being disciplined, and finding the leverage are all vital parts of negotiating. Sometimes there needs to be compromise, sometimes from both sides, and just as importantly a willingness from both sides to do a deal. But if that's the case, the key is to find a genuine "win–win" situation, or the closest possible to a "win–win" that suits all parties. That can then, in some cases, be a positive foundation for a long-standing business relationship.

There is a lot to consider before pursuing international trade, not just in terms of whether it is a good idea but also in terms of how you may wish to approach it. For example:

- Have the goods or service the business offers truly shown high demand in domestic markets? This is something to assess honestly. If there is proven and ideally sustained demand for your good or service, then that shows proof of concept. Having a healthy profit margin is also an important consideration here. However, if it is not the case that there is real high demand at the time, that is not necessarily a reason to abandon the idea of international trade altogether. It may just mean holding off until you have a better idea of the proof of concept.
- Is there sufficient demand for the goods/services that you offer in other countries? This can be tricky to estimate in some

cases and you may have to go with the most informed guess possible, with the information you have available at the time. The critical starting point will be having a reasonable proof of concept in your domestic market as a gauge, as in most cases it is preferable to have good foundation for your business domestically before committing time and resources to selling abroad.

- What will it cost to trade internationally? This can be in terms of tariffs and taxes or increased bureaucracy, outsourcing, and staffing costs and will largely depend on which countries you wish to start trading with. It will be important to ensure that there is balance here and to have a full understanding of what your costs may look like. So, what you will potentially make in terms of income has to make the increased outgoings worth the investment.

- Is your business prepared for international trade? Does your business have the staff and the expertise within to organize, manage, and deal with all of the elements that international trade will bring? Setting this up can be similar in some ways to the initial start-up phase as it is standing up a new part of the business operation. The reality is that trading inter-nationally can be (and probably will be) different and more resource intensive than domestic trading. So, in itself this can be very time consuming and having the resources to do this and keep the domestic business running smoothly is a key issue. Another area to consider is how dynamic your business is and how flexible it is to change as international trade is another area that can be subject to planned and unplanned (sometimes unexpected) change that can directly or indirectly affect your business. If you are unsure about any of these areas, again, it is not necessarily a reason not to proceed, but it is worth considering and ensuring that your business operation is as prepared as it can be for this type of new trading.

- What are the barriers to trade? This will vary depending on what you are trading and which country or countries you want to trade with. Broadly speaking, there are three major barriers to trade. First, natural barriers: These can be physical or cultural. For example, physical distance between countries, which could cause logistical issues transporting goods or language barriers, creating difficulty in negotiating deals and communication. An example of this could be if you outsource clothing manufacturing to an outsource company abroad, language barriers can cause a barrier in negotiations and time management can influence how often you can fly out to check progress and that in turn can leave you open to quality issues. Second, nontariff barriers: These can include import quotas of certain goods, embargoes, exchange controls, and buy national regulations, where privileges are given to domestic manufacturers and retailers. Third, tariff barriers: A tariff is a tax imposed by a nation on imported goods. It can be a charge per unit, a percentage of the value of goods, or in some cases a combination. No matter how they are assessed; the purpose of tariffs is to make imports more expensive and therefore less competitive with domestic product. All of these issues can be factored into your plans, but it is important to know what they are beforehand. It can be a nasty surprise if you have spent time thinking about trading abroad but have not considered tariffs.

- Have you done your research? As outlined in this chapter, there are many areas to research and consider before deciding whether trading internationally is the right decision for your business. It can bring obvious and enormous benefits for any business, but to maximize those benefits and to minimize the (potentially large) risks, it is important to be as fully informed as possible.

So, while it is important to do your research as far as is possible, there is also a need to expect and to prepare as best as you possibly can for the unexpected in the area of international trade. In a lot of cases, many entrepreneurs may have limited experience of trading with other countries, so a fair amount of learning will be done as you go along.

This is an exciting area and can take your business to a new level, and as with many areas of entrepreneurship, proper planning prevents poor performance.

Foreign trade clearly holds down the costs of the products we buy.
—Tim Bishop

CHAPTER 14

Conclusions

The most successful entrepreneurs I know are optimistic. It's part of the job description.

—Caterina Fake

In this book, we have outlined many of the areas an entrepreneur would need to consider from the initial start-up stage, establishing your business to the various possibilities for growth and expansion. Deciding to start your own business does not have any prerequisites, such as a degree or a certain type of education. There are many well-known and very successful entrepreneurs started without any formal qualifications and built some of the world's most successful businesses.

However, in each case, they each had one thing in common. They all started with an idea and the desire, drive, and determination to give it a go, accepting the potential rewards and challenges that will be on the road to success.

As has been covered in this book, there are a lot of areas to consider. Some that you may have thought about, some that may be areas that hadn't been considered or completely new ideas.

Following is a summary of the key messages from the chapters in this book, which could be used as a checklist and help with your informed decision about your business and your options for expansion.

In the world of entrepreneurship and business, and due to the fact that every individual and business is unique, there are so many variables that it is impossible to list every single thing and it's also true to say that you don't have to be an expert in everything. However, having a good idea of your starting point, where you want to go and how you plan to get there, can only be positive.

Chapter 1

- Which entrepreneurs inspire you and why?
- What has inspired you to start your entrepreneurial journey and what do you want to achieve with your business?

Chapter 2

- What is your business idea?
- Is it something completely new and unique or is it something that already exists but you want to present and deliver in a better way?
- What will you call your business?
- If it's something new, such as a new product, will you need to protect your idea?
- Is there a demand for your product or service? Is it scalable?
- How will you setup your business and what do you need to get started?
- How strong is your business network and do you need to expand/strengthen it?
- Will the entrepreneurial lifestyle suit you?

Chapter 3

- Do you plan to grow? Whatever your short-term aims, it will benefit everyone if you have a business with a strong foundation.
- How do you plan to grow? There is more than one way, and some will suit your business model more than others.
- Is growth right for your business and for you?
- What are your criteria for growth? Have you or will you hit those criteria?

Chapter 4

- Who are your key internal and external stakeholders?
- How will you manage and prioritize each of your stakeholders?

- Will these relationships change if you grow your business? If so, how will they change?

Chapter 5

- Are you used to constant change, and can you and your business adapt in an efficient way?
- Have you managed change before, and can you lead your business through it?

Chapter 6

- Have you defined what success looks like and how you plan to get there?
- Do you have a short-, medium-, and long-term plan in place? Is it adaptable?
- How will those plans change when you factor in growth?

Chapter 7

- What is your social media strategy? Is it appropriate for your business model?
- Do you have your own website?
- Are both your social media strategy and website ready for growth? Do you have the resource to manage increased traffic?
- How effective is your networking strategy?
- How will you prioritize your networking events?

Chapter 8

- Do you have a marketing plan, and have you prioritized who you want to reach as potential customers or clients?
- What types of marketing strategies will you use to reach your audience?

Chapter 9

- What finances do you need to make a start on your business and to fund expansion?
- Is your balance sheet looking healthy? If not, what steps could you take to change?
- Does your balance sheet make your business look ready for growth?
- Do you need external funding for your expansion?
- Where will you get these resources?

Chapter 10

- Have you thought through a plan for expansion (possibly a SWOT analysis)?
- Have you fully considered the advantages and disadvantages of growing your business? (There will be both and it is a matter of striking a balance to decide the best way forward.)

Chapter 11

- What resources do you need to run and expand your business?
- Where will you get these resources, and have you prioritized where the most important areas are?
- In the scenario of growth, will you need to reorganize and reprioritize your resources? If so, how will you do this efficiently and effectively?

Chapter 12

- Have you considered your tax and national insurance contributions?
- If you need to recruit staff, how will you do it? How will you manage payroll?
- Have you thought about all of the key areas of cash flow management—for example, managing late payments?

Chapter 13

- Is trading with other countries part of your expansion plans?
- Have you researched the relationship your home country has with the country or countries you wish to trade with?
- Can you realistically resource trading with other countries? If you are not able to currently, how can you achieve it in the future?

So, in overall conclusion, it is fair to say that there is a lot to consider. Running your own business comes with many opportunities for success and challenges along the journey. In the world of entrepreneurship, there isn't an exact science as such, there are too many variables. It cannot be stressed enough that every business and entrepreneur is unique. But if you do your research and consider the many areas that need consideration (sometimes constant consideration), then you undoubtedly will be maximizing your chances of success.

Whether you are currently an entrepreneur, thinking of starting your own business, expanding, or somewhere in between, I hope you have enjoyed reading and wish you every success.

You will either step forward into growth or step back into safety.
—Abraham Maslow

Bibliography

ASEAN. 2021. "About ASEAN." Available at https://asean.org/asean/about-asean/ (accessed July 2021).

BBC. 2021. "Brexit and What You Need to Know." Available at www.bbc.co.uk/news/uk-politics-32810887 (accessed July 2021).

Britannica. 2021. "North American Free Trade Agreement." Available at www.britannica.com/event/North-American-Free-Trade-Agreement (accessed June 2021).

COMESA. 2021. "Overview of COMESA." Available at www.comesa.int/what-is-comesa/ (accessed July 2021).

EFTA. 2021. "Frequently Asked Questions." Available at www.efta.int/About-EFTA/Frequently-asked-questions-EFTA-EEA-EFTA-membership-and-Brexit-328676 (accessed June 2021).

European Union. 2021. "Goals and Values of the EU." Available at https://europa.eu/european-union/about-eu/eu-in-brief_en (accessed June 2021).

Facebook. 2022. "Manchester United Facebook Page." Available at www.facebook.com/manchesterunited/ (accessed January 2022).

Facebook. 2022. "Nike Facebook Page." Available at www.facebook.com/nike/ (accessed January 2022).

Facebook. 2012. "About Facebook. 1 Billion Active Users." Available at www.facebook.com/pg/facebook/about/?ref=page_internal (accessed February 2021).

FBB Publications. 2016. "Social Media—How to Use Social Media Marketing to Grow Your Business." FBB Publications.

Instagram. 2022. "FC Barcelona Official Instagram Page." Available at www.instagram.com/fcbarcelona/ (accessed January 2022).

Instagram. 2022. "Disney Official Instagram Page." Available at www.instagram.com/disney/ (accessed January 2022).

Instagram. 2022. "Arnold Schwarzenegger Official Instagram Page." Available at www.instagram.com/schwarzenegger/ (accessed January 2022).

James, D., and O. James. 2017. *Dynamic Business Environments*. Surrey. Haremi.

James, O., and D. James. 2019. *The Entrepreneurial Adventure: Embracing Risk, Change and Uncertainty*. New York, NY: BEP.

LinkedIn. 2021. "About LinkedIn." Available at https://about.linkedin.com/ (accessed March 2021).

Mercosur. 2021. "Mercosur in Brief." Available at https://www.mercosur.int/en/ (accessed July 2021).

New York Time. 2019. "How TikTok is Rewriting the World." Available at www.nytimes.com/2019/03/10/style/what-is-tik-tok.html (accessed January 2022).

Pacific Alliance. 2021. "What is the Pacific Alliance?" Available at https://alianzapacifico.net/en/what-is-the-pacific-alliance/ (accessed July 2021).

Simply business .2021. SME's. Available at www.simplybusiness.co.uk/knowledge/articles/2020/05/what-is-an-sme/ (accessed February 2021).

Statista. 2021. "Distribution of Instagram Users." Available at www.statista.com/statistics/325587/instagram-global-age-group/ (accessed March 2021).

Tutor 2 you. 2021. "What is a Trading Bloc?" Available at www.tutor2u.net/business/reference/what-is-a-trading-bloc (accessed April 2021).

Twitter. 2022. "Lord Alan Sugar Official Twitter Page." Available at https://twitter.com/Lord_Sugar (accessed January 2022).

Twitter. 2022. "Mark Cuban Official Twitter Page." Available at https://twitter.com/mcuban (accessed January 2022).

Twitter. 2022. "Starbucks Official Twitter Page." Available at https://twitter.com/Starbucks (accessed January 2022).

UK Government. 2019. "Patents, Trademarks, Copyright and Designs." Available at https://www.gov.uk/browse/business/intellectual-property (accessed January 2020).

United Nations. 2021. SAFTA. Available at https://www.un.org/ldcportal/south-asian-free-trade-area/ (accessed July 2021).

What Franchise—Starbucks. n.d. Available at www.what-franchise.com/franchise-opportunities/coffee-franchises/starbucks-coffee-franchisee (accessed January 2020).

Which Franchise. 2019. "Which Franchise." Available at www.whichfranchise.com/ (accessed January 2020).

YouTube. 2022. "PewDiePie Official YouTube Page." Available at www.youtube.com/user/PewDiePie (accessed January 2022).

YouTube. 2022. "Jenna Marbles Official YouTube Page." Available at www.youtube.com/user/JennaMarbles (accessed January 2022).

About the Author

Oliver James currently works for DJ Learning Ltd., and is responsible for day-to-day operations, supplier relationships, and networking.

This is his second publication for Business Expert Press, having previously coauthored *The Entrepreneurial Adventure: Embracing Risk, Change, and Uncertainty.*

He has worked on the design of two MOOCs (Professional Skills for International Business and Management Skills for International Business) for the University of London and coauthored a book *Dynamic Business Environments* for another client and publisher.

He previously worked for a big telecommunication company in various roles, including team leadership and project management, and worked in India on two separate occasions, successfully delivering complex change projects.

In his spare time, he is a mentor for the Prince's trust and works with Careers Wales doing mock interviews and careers talks at 6th Form's. In addition to this, he volunteers for a dog rescue shelter, and he also enjoys long-distance running, including the London Marathon four times, raising money for Children with Cancer UK.

Index

OTHER TITLES IN THE ENTREPRENEURSHIP AND SMALL BUSINESS MANAGEMENT COLLECTION

Scott Shane, Case Western University, Editor

- *The Entrepreneurial Adventure* by David Roemer
- *Building Business Capacity* by Sheryl Hardin
- *The Startup Master Plan* by Nikhil Agarwal and Krishiv Agarwal
- *Managing Health and Safety in a Small Business* by Jacqueline Jeynes
- *Modern Devil's Advocacy* by Robert Koshinskie
- *Dead Fish Don't Swim Upstream* by Silverberg Jay
- *The 8 Superpowers of Successful Entrepreneurs* by Marina Nicholas
- *Founders, Freelancers & Rebels* by Helen Jane Campbell
- *Time Management for Unicorns* by Giulio D'Agostino
- *Zero to $10 Million* by Shane Brett
- *Navigating the New Normal* by Rodd Mann
- *Ethical Business Culture* by Andreas Karaoulanis
- *Blockchain Value* by Olga V. Mack
- *TAP Into Your Potential* by Rick De La Guardia
- *Stop, Change, Grow* by Michael Carter and Karl Shaikh
- *Dynastic Planning* by Walid S. Chiniara

Concise and Applied Business Books

The Collection listed above is one of 30 business subject collections that Business Expert Press has grown to make BEP a premiere publisher of print and digital books. Our concise and applied books are for…

- Professionals and Practitioners
- Faculty who adopt our books for courses
- Librarians who know that BEP's Digital Libraries are a unique way to offer students ebooks to download, not restricted with any digital rights management
- Executive Training Course Leaders
- Business Seminar Organizers

Business Expert Press books are for anyone who needs to dig deeper on business ideas, goals, and solutions to everyday problems. Whether one print book, one ebook, or buying a digital library of 110 ebooks, we remain the affordable and smart way to be business smart. For more information, please visit www.businessexpertpress.com, or contact sales@businessexpertpress.com.

www.ingramcontent.com/pod-product-compliance
Lightning Source LLC
Chambersburg PA
CBHW061317220326
41599CB00026B/4916